LETS
GO
PUBLISH!

Dedication

I dedicate this book

To my wonderful brothers and sisters:

Angel Edward J. Kelly, Jr.

Nancy "Ann" Flannery

Mary A. Daniels

Joseph A. Kelly

I surely am a lucky person to have

Such wonderfulness in the family of

Edward J Kelly and Irene McKeown Kelly

.

Acknowledgments:

I appreciate all the help that I have received in putting this book together as well as all of the other 172 books from the past.

My acknowledgments were so large at one time that readers complained that they had to go through too many pages to get to page one.

And, so I put my acknowledgment list online, and it continues to grow. Believe it or not, it now costs about a dollar less to print my books. No kidding!

Thank you and God bless you all for your help. Please check out www.letsgopublish.com to read the latest version of my heartfelt acknowledgments updated for this book.

In this book, I received some extra special help from many fine American patriots including Dennis Grimes, Gerry Rodski, Wily Ky Eyely, Angel Irene McKeown Kelly, Angel Edward Joseph Kelly Sr., Angel Edward Joseph Kelly Jr., Ann Flannery, Angel James Flannery Sr., Mary Daniels, Bill Daniels, Angel Robert Gary Daniels, Angel Sarah Janice Daniels, Angel Punkie Daniels, Joe Kelly, Diane Kelly, Brian P. Kelly, Mike P. Kelly, Katie P. Kelly, Angel Ben Kelly, Budmund (Buddy) Arthur Kelly, and Seamus Arthur McDuff!

Thank you all!

Table of Contents

Dedication v

Table of Contents ix

Chapter 1 Answer to the Title Statement: 1

Chapter 2 What Do Regular Americans Think? 3

Chapter 3 Whites Fought Whites for Black Freedom 11

Chapter 4 Where Did All the Hate Come From? 17

Chapter 5 Off the Wall Groups and Schools 29

Chapter 6 Is Donald Trump White? 39

Chapter 7 Not Your Father's Democratic Party 53

Chapter 8 Solving Problem 60 Million Illegal Interlopers ... 59

Chapter 9 Are Whites Being Left Behind in America? 63

Chapter 10 Hating Whitey 73

Chapter 11 Trump's Angry White Men 81

Chapter 12 Most Politicians Are Still White Men 87

Chapter 13 No Borders; No Wall; No USA At All 95

Chapter 14 Final: Why Nation Must Choose Civility 109

Other Books by Brian Kelly: (amazon.com, and Kindle) 115

Preface:

For the new book *White People are Bad! Bad! Bad!*

Most white people are amazed that they are now the subject of verbal abuse and attacks from disgruntled lefties across the United States. Lefties have still not gotten over their loss in the 2016 election and so they are lashing out at white folks to help them feel better. Liberal Progressive Democrats have nothing better to do than pick on Whitey and show their hate simply because the preponderance of the Republicans, including Trump, the election victor, are White.

Whites are taking solace in new slogans like "It's OK to be white," (IOTBW). This little ditty is based on a poster campaign organized on the American imageboard *4chan* in 2017. Originally, it was a "proof of concept" that a "harmless message" would cause a "massive media shitstorm", so that the media backlash against the slogan would help convert white Americans to the far-right. Regular Americans have not been moved and are not way, way right

According to The Concise Oxford Dictionary of Politics, in liberal democracies; the political right opposes socialism and social democracy. Right-wing parties include conservatives, Christian democrats, classical liberals, nationalists and on the very far-right; racists and fascists. Regular White folks are not far right but you can't convince hateful leftists and hateful Democrat Progressives of that. Republicans are not far right either. Unfortunately, for the Republican Party, their RINOS are not even conservative.

The IOTBW was implemented with posters and stickers containing the sentence "It's OK to be white" being placed in streets in the United States as well as on college campuses in the United States, Canada, New Zealand, Australia and the United Kingdom. Like all things perhaps intending no harm, harm came from it anyway as the slogan was spread according to the proof of concept by neo-Nazis, and racist groups including white supremists. Nonetheless it is a great saying for regular white folk who simply want life to be OK and they don't want thugs and imbeciles picking on them for any reason. .

When the major hate thought from the media and the Democrats is *White People Are Bad! Bad! Bad!* and the corrupt press and the Democrats find that perfectly acceptable, why shouldn't regular people who are conservatives, but not whackos, have a comeback phrase that says, "It is OK to be White!"

Actually, it is OK to be White, Black, Yellow, Red or Brown. Why should it matter?

Nonetheless, small minds find fault with many things. In November 2017, Lucian Wintrich attempted to give a speech titled "It's OK to Be White" at the University of Connecticut as an invited speaker of the school's Republican Club. The speech was protested and came to an end when a protester, employed as the director of career services at Quinebaug Valley Community College, grabbed Wintrich's speech papers from the podium and Wintrich grabbed her, hoping to rescue his papers, resulting in breach of peace charges against Wintrich. The left is never guilty because they lie, and the media swears to it.

Have we really reached the point where saying it's okay to be a certain race is what people consider racism? This is beyond reason. It's so sad. How would people react to see posters saying that it is OK to be Black? It is OK to be anything except a danger to somebody else.

My father, a white Brewery worker taught me when I was growing up in Pennsylvania that I should look at people as individuals, not through a racial lens. Just as it was wrong for white racists to hate black people, it is just as wrong for Blacks to hate white people. Saying Whites, Reds, Blacks, Yellows or Browns are bad is wrong, period.

Thus, it is wrong to say *Whites are Bad*! Yes, it is OK to be White and it is OK for a beholder to be proud of their whiteness. Same for Black, Red, Yellow, and Brown. All the noise is just a clanging by hatemongers with little else to do.

You are going to love this book. Pick it up and you won't put it down.

There are many of us who, after crying out for relief for our country for eight long years, believe in our hearts that God's answer to our cries is Donald Trump. It is up to US now to make sure we make the most of God's great gift. And, yes, Trump happens to be White and he is OK with that and holds no animus towards other races.

I knew that I was voting for Donald Trump as soon as he broke through the pack of Republicans and began his showdowns with his real opponent, Hillary Clinton. Like many Democrats, I had had enough of Obama and the Clintons, but my predilection to Trump was more because of him and not because of Clinton negatives. It had more to do with the fact that he reminded me of a last man standing in the way of a country ready to go off a big cliff. Trump has already prevented a big American Doomsday.

At the end of the day, when the dust had settled, and the battle was over, the last man standing won. Donald Trump won the election despite all odds. In many ways he got elected because he was the last man standing between an Obama-like American hell-hole and a return to the Promised Land of our founders. To this day liberal progressive socialist Democrats have been sore losers and they are not willing to put in a quiet eight years. They want the people who duly elected a great president to pay dearly for their vote because it was against what Democrats had ordered.

"Millions of Americans," declared Dallas megachurch pastor Robert Jeffries in 2017, "believe the election of President Trump represented God giving us another chance—perhaps our last chance—to truly make America great again. Our job was to elect him once God showed us the way. We thank Our Lord to this day that we did."

Donald Trump got elected because someone whispered into the individual ears of millions of Americans—Whites and Blacks, and other ethnicities, Catholics and Protestants, Muslims and Jews, and those of many persuasions that together in this election, we could all make a difference, and then Donald Trump would be that difference. The people trusted this self-made Billionaire to do what was best for America and not the bidding of slimy grease-ball politicians or political donors, rats, and hacks.

For the Whites that get slammed as being bad! bad! bad! Mr. Trump was the only candidate for president who offered Americans a breath of fresh air from the stodgy, bossy, establishment elites in both the Democratic and Republican Parties. Trump defied the status quo of rich donors controlling the government for their personal benefit. Donald Trump to many, including myself, is one of the greatest gifts of all-time from God himself. Whites are not bad! bad! bad! Whites are not even bad.

Trump is white but that does not matter at all to Whites who were hoping the first black President would act like Trump acts in terms of getting things done for America and Americans. If Obama represented the same welcome change from establishment elitist politics, I am convinced he would have been received positively by white males in either party. Trump's great ideas for solving the issues facing America today line up with the thinking of most Americans who are paying attention and who were annoyed at the lack of results and the lack of effort from the prior administration.

I am glad that you are reading this book, so you too can understand why it is OK to be White even though there are a lot of Democrats acting as jerks trying to put the idea of whiteness down.

Donald Trump was not just a default choice for President. I wrote an essay early in the campaign titled, God gave us Donald Trump. I stood by that thought even after the Democrats continued to add Russian characters into their daily soap opera trying to replay and undo the 2016 election. Dirty Democrat shenanigans are getting old, don't you think? Damning Whites is just another of their dirty tricks. I have never been more pleased with a vote than my vote for Donald J. Trump. Thank you, Dear Lord. Please let the dirty Democrats see the light.

Trump is a great man, who happens to be white. He is already becoming a great president for you, me, and all those who love America. Those who do not love America need to find a place to go and get there without hurting this country any more than they already have.

Trump knows business and we are already experiencing an enlivened economy. With substantial foreign business experience, he is setting

America up as the top dog in the world, and as expected, he is making no apologies. Whites need to take a lesson from Trump: Make no apologies for America and none for your Whiteness.

Trump is a tough American, so we can count on not being pushed around in foreign affairs or delicate negotiations. Our new president as expected, is a winner all the way around. He loves helping all Americans win. He hates to lose and seldom does. America is very happy that we now have someone in charge who believes we can win.

The weaknesses of the Republican Party came out in spades in the primary season and continued as weak-kneed RINOs such as Jeb Bush, John Kasich, Carly Fiorina, George Pataki, Marco Rubio, and John McCain decided to become tools for the Democrats. During the campaign Donald Trump did not even give them lip service.

In his own way, Mr. Trump told them and all the establishment elites where to go. I like that. I suspect God will get them there eventually. These RINOs and their Progressive Marxist friends across the aisle had been destroying America for their own benefit. It took a guy with guts and stamina to beat them. The last man standing stood against them and won a great victory for the people.

Donald Trump first whooped everybody who was anybody in the GOP. He then ran against a person that some call a withered fascist-- Hillary Clinton. There were many Democrats like me who felt that we could not afford a liar in the White House. We were all in for Donald J. Trump. People in my own family who were Democrats for years, switched to Republican so they too could vote for Trump in the PA Primary.

For those who can ignore the media's fake news and outright lies, there is plenty to admire about President Trump. His whiteness is simply an attribute and it is not a negative. Watching his children in action at the GOP convention and the chemistry within the Trump family, Americans got the full sense of what a fine man and a fine dad he is.

America needs Donald Trump—a businessman and a great negotiator for our country to compete in the world. We could not make it with a guy such as our former president who unfortunately for the country found business as a necessary unpleasant evil. Barack Obama chose to have nothing to do with sound business principles while being in charge of the US economy. Hillary Clinton was ready to be more of the same—a third Term of Obama.

Whether he did or not, the former president gave the impression for years that he had true disdain for America and Americans. It was like he would have loved all Americans to give up their freedoms and become government dependents. I am convinced that he would have liked America to give up its position as #1 in the world to give other countries more of a chance to beat us. Trump is clearly for America and Americans-First and he demonstrated that in his nearly 400 huge campaign rallies. Trump is a Nationalist / Populist who ran as a Republican because it made business sense to not go third party.

Hillary was more like Obama -- socialistic and Marxist and she came off even more radical than Obama. For example, Hillary never seemed to be too keen on freedom. She likes her freedom for sure but not yours. She was working on eliminating the Bill of Rights and had already earmarked the #1 and #2 Amendments of the Constitution for removal.

Yes, we were at the point in our history in which a presidential candidate's position of not being actively opposed to the Bill of Rights was a key selling point for their candidacy.

The GOP today is still full of losers and babies who won't even keep their vows made in the pledge to support the Party's own nominee. No wonder the prior president was treated as an emperor. His sad agenda received no interference from the wimpy GOP. The scaredy-cat RINOS quaked at the sight of Obama. Then they became Never-Trampers. To me, they are all losers—especially the Bushes and Marco Rubio, Billy Kristol and George Will. Trump doesn't quake at anything. In fact, he makes me proud to be an American

For years, I have hoped that somebody such as Rush Limbaugh or Donald Trump or somebody with influence and power and money would come along to change our two-party system. I put my vision to words in two books, the first, written five years ago titled, Kill the Republican Party, and the second written in the summer of 2017, titled It's Time for the John Doe Party.

The idea is to rid the Republican Party of the swamp and start over again with a new name such as The American Party or The John Doe Party, hoping to attract all current Republican regular people— the 89% who today favor Trump, leaving the RINOS, the Never Trampers, and the Swamp behind. I think the new Party would attract all Democrats who are like me--pro-American to a fault. It is still a dream yet for many like me as we are watching the disappointing Republican Congress very closely We are very unhappy with Swamp rats such as Paul Ryan and Mitch McConnell, who have ignored the people for way too many years.

For this ole conservative Democrat, the Republicans for years—even when my dad and I voted together before he died, always seemed to be the better choice than the far-left whacko Democrats. Yet, after Reagan, there were too many bad choices and too many weak men.

Donald Trump has a lot of Reagan toughness and goodness in him. He has a great plan for America and in this book, we defend all the good people, especially the Whites who are the reasons for "Why Trump Got Elected!" Besides being favored by God, and maybe that alone is enough, first of all, Trump was and still is the best choice. Second, he is honest. Third, he has kept his word about making America great again in ways in which Americans will all be so pleased.

Despite the squawking about his tweets and his social life as a wild young man. Trump is destined to be a great President. In my prayers I ask the Lord to take care of him so that he can provide for America for many years and set us up for another good leader when his eight years are up. I am convinced that his whiteness will not get in his way.

America has had more than one economic issue for sure, but it still is the best place to live on earth. People from all over the world flock to our shores because there is no better place to live even though Democrat Andrew Cuomo says that America was never that great!

When Donald Trump was inaugurated, our nation was full to the brim with economic issues. When tackled one by one, they are now being solved and right now, there are many positive works in process—things are being solved thanks to the new President.

This book reminds us of the disdain Democrats have for the Trump victory and for the people, even the Democrats, who voted for him. Those voters, White, Black, and other will remember the hate Democrats have for us and they shall not get our votes again. This book again reminds us that the Obama years prevented many people in American from having a good life.

Donald Trump and Mike Pence have taken on the mission to make life better for all Americans. Trump had a good life before becoming President. He did not have to help us. He does not need the job. I am so glad he is the President. I bet God whispered in his ear to get him moving, putting all his gifts together to help America. Thank you, God. Thank you, Donald Trump.

I sure hope you enjoy this book and I hope that it inspires you to continue to take action. Our Congress can certainly be more pro-American and more responsive to the people's needs and not their own. Let's get rid of Democrats like Matt Cartwright and Bob Casey Jr. from Pennsylvania and other weak people in our Congress. I hope the book in some ways helps you look at things differently. Keep your whiteness in its right place and make room for all colors in your life. Don't let the leftists intimidate you.

Our new president has settled in and he is already implementing a host of innovative items on his agenda. I hope you digest Trump's entire plan, be willing to adopt it, and add to it your own positive notions for building a better America. And, please do not trust the press to do your thinking for you.

Together, we, Black and White and Yellow and Brown and Red, and others can help make the US a far better country. We should smile as we have already accomplished our first and best objective with more to come. We elected Donald Trump as our president. Now, we must support his hard work by electing the people who will help him help America and we must speak up to the Congress whenever they get in our President's way.

Thank you

Brian W. Kelly, Author

About the Author

Brian W. Kelly is a retired Assistant Professor in the Business Information Technology (BIT) program at Marywood University, where he also served as the IBM i and midrange systems technical advisor to the IT faculty. Kelly developed and taught many college and professional courses in the IT and business areas. He is also a contributing technical editor to IT Jungle's "The Four Hundred" and "Four Hundred Guru" Newsletters.

A former IBM Senior Systems Engineer, he has an active consultancy in the information technology field, (www.kellyconsulting.com). He is the author of 172 other books and hundreds of articles about IT and topics about America.

Book # 173 is called White People Are Bad! Bad! Bad! and it has a number of suggestions that when added to Trump's own, will help Make America Great Again.

Kelly is a frequent speaker at US events such as COMMON, IBM conferences, and other technical conferences and computer user group meetings across the United States. Brian is always ready to accept invitations to speak at political rallies on behalf of conservative and nationalist candidates.

Brian ran for Congress as a conservative Democrat in 2010, took no donations, and shook up the political world in Northeastern PA when he scored 17% of the vote in a three man-race.

Chapter 1 Answer to the Title Statement:

White People Are Bad! Bad! Bad!

Like Hell!

Chapter 2 What Do Regular Americans Think?

Whitey & Discrimination?

A new NY Times Editorial Staff member Sarah Jeong was in the news a lot the first week of August 2018 because she is an avowed racist by her actions. Here are two of her tweets from the recent past:

1. "#cancelwhitepeople."

2 "White people have stopped breeding. you'll all go extinct soon. that was my plan all along."

Sweet, don't you think?

Racist?

See how sweet she looks in the picture to the left. Sometimes a picture is deceiving. Plus, there is a new wrinkle in the notion about who in the US actually can rightfully be included as a racist. Because she is as an Asian (minority), current Democratic thinking is that she cannot be a racist.

According to popular Democrat Jesse Jackson when he picked on Whites in his 1989-ish run for the Presidency, he set the standard that she and many other leftists believe. Dr. Al Sharpton is another proponent of the philosophy that only Whites can be racist.

A majority of Whites say discrimination against them most certainly exists in America today. This verdict has been captured by many pollsters, most recently , it was the clear sentiment in a poll released recently from NPR, the Robert Wood Johnson Foundation and the Harvard T.H. Chan School of Public Health.

Here is what they say: "If you apply for a job, they seem to give the Blacks the first crack at it," said 68-year-old Tim Hershman of Akron, Ohio, "and, basically, you know, if you want any help from the government, if you're white, you don't get it. If you're black, you get it." Why do white people such as Tim and many others feel that way? Because it is true!

More than half of Whites — 55 percent — surveyed say that, generally speaking, they believe there is discrimination against white people in America today. Hershman's view is similar to what was heard on the campaign trail at Trump rally after Trump rally. Donald Trump catered to this white grievance during the 2016 presidential campaign and has done so as president as well. There is no place for racism in America but somehow Whitey has been left out of all the areas which offer protection from such abuse.

President Trump speaks to a crowd of supporters at the Phoenix Convention Center during a rally on Aug. 22, 2017 --- Photo by *Ralph Freso/Getty Images*

Tough Trump is a favorite of conservative Whites, recent polls show a huge grouping of Blacks of all persuasions checking out what Trump has to offer and liking it.

Notable, of course in all of this is that while a majority of Whites in the poll say discrimination against them exists It is also important to note is that 84 percent of Whites believe discrimination exists against racial and ethnic minorities in America today. The Whites that I know think that all such discrimination id bad.

Why is it that this obvious open racism against Whites is so prevalent today that grandma and grandpa in their rocking chairs are noticing it? Well, besides the fact that grandma and grandpa while in those rocking chairs are listening to Talk Radio and tuning in to many TV programs that demonstrate that the days of the majority Whites being treated as the majority in the country are over. Vocal minorities, hate groups, and the Democratic Party have seen to that. For whatever reason white males in the Democratic Party do not identify as the White Bad Guys!

Logic dictates that there is nothing intrinsically wrong with white males, or for that matter white females, despite the many aspersions cast the White Way in recent times, the same goes for any other race.

By the way, Wikipedia, mostly disrespected by coffee breath professors often gives great sourced information. It delivers are far richer discussion of relevant topics and is quite a bit more than the 1960's Cliffs-Notes mini versions of major works.

Wikipedia thus does not deserve the stain placed on it by pure academicians. The following paragraph is from Wikipedia and it shows how from ancient times, mankind has divided people into categories or characteristics. Whites and Blacks are two such categories.

"Identifying human races in terms of skin color, at least as one among several physiological characteristics, has been common since antiquity. Via rabbinical literature, the division is received in early modern scholarship, mostly in four to five categories. It was long recognized that the number of categories is arbitrary and subjective.

François Bernier(1684) doubted the validity of using skin color as a racial characteristic, and Charles Darwin emphasized the gradual differences between categories. The most influential division is due to Johann Friedrich Blumenbach (1779), which divides mankind into "Caucasian or White", "Mongolian or Yellow", "Aethiopian or Black", "American or Copper-colored" and "Malayan or Olive-colored" subgroups."

The main stream, aka lamestream, aka drive-by media—lie, and the "journalists" associated with their ilk swear to it. And the Grey Lady, the once respected New York Times, just signaled to the rest of the world with its new hire that it is OK to hire racists, as long as they are not male and not white. It is part of the not so new popular cult religion called Leftism.

Of course, as definitions change it gets more and more difficult to know where anybody stands on anything. For example, there was a time that the popular Merriam-Webster dictionary defined "liberal" as being "not opposed to new ideas or ways of behaving that are not traditional or widely accepted."

To most, Leftists and liberals used to mean the same thing. The terminology was simple- left-wingers are liberal, right-wingers are conservative. Liberals are open to new trends in society, while conservatives are more comfortable with tradition.

But nowadays, Leftism has become a rigid ideology of its own. It does not subscribe to the traditional progressive ideology but rather has carved out its own. No more are they liberal in the traditional sense, which boils down to "live and let live." Instead, they believe that anyone that doesn't agree with hard Leftist ideology is evil and must be excommunicated. That is why there is such great division in the country. In times past, it would not be accepted to mock Whites as bad! bad! bad! Without making a major case with all points proven. Not today!

It is easy to get the feeling, and I for one do get the feeling from listening to and watching the daily soap opera of the drive-by media that it is not very fashionable to be a man these days, especially a white man. It is just not a good thing, so it seems. When I get up in the morning, I look and there it is, a man looking a lot like me with a definite case of terminal whiteness staring right back at me.

Please let me interject an appropriate poem that talks about self-esteem, White or Black, and what it is all about. I may have terminal whiteness and I am proud of it. When I look at the man in the glass, it gives me cause for a big smile. Here is the timeless poem by Dale Wimbrow from 1934. My McKeown relatives on my mother's side insist and perhaps rightly so that my Uncle Nick McKeown wrote this poem as he recited it so frequently and so fluently.

THE MAN IN THE GLASS

When you get what you want in your struggle for self
And the world makes you king for a day,
Just go to a mirror and look at yourself
And see what THAT man has to say.

For it isn't your father or mother or wife
Whose judgment upon you must pass,
The fellow whose verdict counts most in your life
Is the one staring back from the glass.

Some people might think you're a straight-shootin' chum
And call you a wonderful guy.
But the man in the glass says you're only a bum
If you can't look him straight in the eye.

He's the fellow to please, never mind all the rest
For he's with you clear to the end
And you've passed the most dangerous test
If the guy in the glass is your friend

You may fool all the world down the pathway of years
And get pats on the back as you pass
But your final reward will be heartache and tears
If you've cheated the man in glass

-- Dale Wimbrow, 1934

Read this poem as often as you may and remember the name callers who are now picking on White people. They too every day must look in the glass

Back to the main thought. Are white people bad? Of course not; but try getting a leftist to agree with you. It's like trying to tie a hair ribbon on a bolt of lightning.

How did it happen that the majority race in the Unites States has become the Rodney Dangerfield of races? There is no respect in the "popular media" or the Democratic Party for anyone of the race Caucasian. Last time I checked, after 70 years on the planet, because I have had nothing to do with the root cause of this recent phenomenon, I take no blame for the misguided perspective of those on the far left. My statistic is lumped in with all other Whites who are part of the majority race.

None of the White males in my inner circle of whom I am aware, every did anything to warrant blame for being among a sect known as "Nasty White Guys" yet we are getting it anyway. If there is blame to dole out, I think it belongs with the real racists and bigots in the media, who are always looking for something bad to blame for mostly anything. Well, don't look my way. It is all balderdash.

Many of us recall when the Me too! movement, which apparently worked well for women of different races and persuasions, found the very White and Jewish Harvey Weinstein as the bad guy for years of apparent sexual assault and harassment. The always racist New York Times ran a hit piece entitled "The unexamined brutality of the male libido" authored by the Canadian writer Stephen Marche.

The article singled out men and the treatment of men by the *Drive-By Media* as being the major reason for all the lying in the world. Marche went on a bit of a diatribe to make his point: "What any given man might say about gender politics and how he treats women are separate and unrelated phenomena. Liberal or conservative, feminist or chauvinist, woke or benighted, young or old, found on Fox News or in The New Republic, a man's stated opinions have next to no relationship to behavior." In other words, the word *male* and the word *lie* have become semi synonyms. Is Stephen a male name? At least there was no color differentiation foisted on men in his hit piece.

Marche continued with a little Freud: "The point of Freud was not that boys will be boys," wrote Marche. "Rather the opposite... If you let boys be boys, they will murder their fathers and sleep with their mothers." And, so lying is not the worst to expect from the sperm carriers of the species.

British Historian and conservative political commentator Nigel Ferguson weighed in with: "Masculinity, not ideology, drives extremist groups," Ferguson went on about a small conference he put together in which he invited five females to participate. None attended and so for that reason alone, he was taken over the coals by the media, in a vitriolic response, because there were no non-Caucasians and no non-males at the conference. The reported story was "Too white and too male,"

The New York Times, not a friend of Americans of any race, but especially hateful against men and Whites, sought to punish Ferguson for running a show with no women. The management published the photographs of all the speakers at the conference (as noted, all male).

The Times' as the literary god and goddess of the world, had as its purpose to shame the presenters for their maleness and their whiteness. According to the Times, those two biggies, whiteness and maleness, had to be the only reasons Ferguson invited them to present at the conference. The Times felt all the white males needed to be shamed for having participated since no women of any color presented. They chose not to accept the invitation, but it was Whitey's fault.

To add a bit more nastiness to the observers of the conference, about a dozen academics — male as well as female — took to social media to call his conference a "StanfordSausageFest." Their raw perspective: "White men are bad, bad bad!" was very evident .White is not even a color. It is in fact, the absence of color and today, color of course is everything. Ask the N Y Times if this is not true for they claim to know everything.

Chapter 3 Whites Fought Whites for Black Freedom

My grade school education was like most.

In the Kelly family, we were all raised to believe in the equal rights of all people, regardless of sex, race, creed, or any other difference left wingers like to highlight. In fact, we only knew of race as it was taught about the Civil War as White guys from North and South fought each other to free Black guys who lived in plantations in the South. It was not taught as a negative per se but as a fact.

At St. Boniface School, the good Sisters of Christian Charity, an order with German heritage, taught us all about the evils of slavery, and the horrors of the Civil War, the war used to end slavery. This war pitted mostly white males from the North against mostly white males from the south in a battle to decide whether slavery would continue and whether the black slaves would be freed . The nuns never really explained the war and its rationale in the type of racist terms used today.

To be exact, there were Blacks who were also engaged in the Civil War on both the Union (North) and Confederate Side. In the Union army, over 179,000 Black men served in over 160 units, as well as more serving in the Navy and in support positions. This number comprised of both northern free African Americans and runaway slaves from the South who enlisted to fight. In the Confederacy, Blacks were not originally free to join the armed services as they were still slaves. Those who did serve were mostly in labor positions. By 1865, the South allowed slaves to enlist but very few actually did.

The Union Army consisted mostly of white soldiers—2,489,836. The Confederate Army consisted also of mostly white soldiers— 1,082,119 . There were 28,000 native Americans who fought in the

Civil War. Just like North and South Whites, Native American families and tribes were often split as for which side they chose to fight.

I cite the Civil War in this chapter as this was, in my opinion, a battle between good white people who did not believe in slavery fighting misguided white people who selfishly enjoyed the benefits of slavery. The good Whites outnumbered the bad Whites and won the war, which ultimately made Black people as free as White people. Not all White people are racists and not all Black people are racists but there are some on both sides. Calling Whitey "Bad! Bad! Bad" is not going to solve the opinion divide.

At St. Boniface K-8 School, there was no racism. The Nuns spent a lot of time talking about how the slave ship business with captains trained in cruelty, busted up African families and with no regard to their humanity. They captured the people—men, women, and children and brought them to America and other areas of the world, such as Europe. They were stolen like property and uprooted from their families to do the bidding of those who would eventually "own them."

The future slaves were brought to America and other lands upon large "Slave ships" which often had been cargo ships. They were specially converted for the purpose of transporting future slaves. Such ships were often known as *Guineamen* because their trade involved trafficking to and from the Guinea coast in West Africa.

The first owners gained the term *slavemasters* for their primary role in the subjugation of these poor people. The term means one who "owns" a slave. *AKA, one who controls the action of a slave owned by others.*

There is no excuse made in this book for slavery. It is an evil practice no matter who does what to whom. Slavery, however, was not limited to White cruelty to Blacks. Slavery and slave trading had been part of European experience long before the beginning of the transatlantic slave trade. It was most widespread in the continuing conflict between Christians and Muslims in the Mediterranean.

There, and around the Black Sea, slaves were created as each side enslaved the other as part of the spoils of war. The numbers were enormous. One cannot see any religion, whether it be Catholic Protestant, or Jewish, or native African religions, condoning slavery. Nonetheless it was practiced by all men—White, Black, and all other colors for centuries. As hard as it may be to believe as late as the mid-17th century, far more European slaves were held in Islamic regions (where the ownership of Muslim slaves was prohibited) than Africans were shipped into the Americas.

Think of the prohibition by Muslims about Muslims. In this instance, they almost had it right.

There was, however, one striking difference to the transatlantic trade: no one really associated slavery with race or color. Slaves could be Black or White, Christian, Muslim or pagan. Moreover, despite the fact that significant slave trading by Arabs to Black Africa had been going on since ancient times, the link between slavery and ethnicity (or, more popularly, 'race') – that is, between slavery and Blackness-was more or less non-existent. However, this form ended when a new "deal" was forged by maritime Europeans in the form of chattel slavery.

To reiterate and clarify. Slavery of course existed in Africa, but it was not the same type of slavery that the Europeans introduced about 500 years ago. The European form was called chattel slavery. A chattel slave is a piece of property, with no rights. ... Slaves in Africa lost the protection of their family and their place in society through enslavement. Europeans added a sinister element to the African idea of slavery. Slaves were actual property who could be bought, sold, traded or inherited.

Whether White v Black or Black v White; whether Black v Black or White v White; whether any color v any color or any type of person v any other type of person, slavery is always wrong. It is also evil and inhuman. It was a poor choice for all practitioners regardless of color, and because of its prevalence, even otherwise good people, White or Black, etc. engaged in slavery practices and believed they were doing no wrong. Over time, all civilized nations, however, recognized the pure evil in all forms of slavery. Bad ideas are not eradicated overnight.

Admittedly, chattel slavery is what most people have in mind when they think of the kind of slavery that existed in the United States before the Civil War, and that existed legally throughout many parts of the world as far back as recorded history. The Civil War in the minds of most people was a way for the majority of White people to eliminate slavery from our country permanently though the stains of slavery in many ways, though muted, still exist. Until recent times, racism, one of the stains of slavery was slowly being minimized as more people accepted differences and even diversity.

Today, however the Democratic Party has reenergized the notion of differences and though they seemingly believe in diversity, if anybody, White or Black, does not march to the full credo of this Party which advocates "hate thy brother," they are simply not welcome. Before Democrat messages about their foes began recently to be laced with intense hate, the time that passed from the 1860's had already made things much better.

The people of America had begun to naturally accept the differences of free people. There were fewer and fewer hate mongers walking among the people. Now, Democrats with the help of a corrupt biased press have set America back to the 1870's, and in a most sinister move, they lie and blame the Republicans for the hate.

Let's finish up this section with a poem that captures the evils of slavery for all men, White and Black alike. Following the poem, I will wrap up my notion of Black and White as taught to me in grade school, and more advanced educational institutions.

The Slave Auction

BY FRANCES ELLEN WATKINS HARPER

The sale began—young girls were there,
   Defenseless in their wretchedness,
Whose stifled sobs of deep despair
   Revealed their anguish and distress.

And mothers stood, with streaming eyes,
   And saw their dearest children sold;
Unheeded rose their bitter cries,
   While tyrants bartered them for gold.

And woman, with her love and truth—
   For these in sable forms may dwell—
Gazed on the husband of her youth,
   With anguish none may paint or tell.

And men, whose sole crime was their hue,
   The impress of their Maker's hand,
And frail and shrinking children too,
   Were gathered in that mournful band.

Ye who have laid your loved to rest,
   And wept above their lifeless clay,
Know not the anguish of that breast,
   Whose loved are rudely torn away.

Ye may not know how desolate
   Are bosoms rudely forced to part,
And how a dull and heavy weight
   Will press the life-drops from the heart.

The Nuns were the first who told us about slaves and slavery in grades 1 thru 8 on Blackman Street Hill. But then there was high school and afterwards, college. Early on those living in Pennsylvania well understood that the human past was characterized by deeds not so noble and discriminations of many kinds. There were signs at one time in my city: "Irish need not apply." Those who settled American cities, were mostly European White and they called the shots.

There were also signs my neighbors in our Syrian neighborhood on High Street, told me that would say, "Syrians need not apply!". There were very few negroes as we called them back then and so I do not know how they were discriminated against, but I suspect they were. It's just how it was. The person who owned the business was the boss.

None of this was news to me or to anybody who payed attention to the lessons of grammar, high school, and college. . We were northerners of course and as white as we were, we were outraged at the very idea of slavery and the cruelness and the evil involved in the slave trade. While hearing these lessons, I do not recall anybody talking about how great and privileged poor white people were simply because we were white and Christian. Just the opposite.

Now I find myself having to look in the mirror every day due to the persistence of a corrupt press to cast blame on all White males to see if I may have gotten a bit darker and thus more pleasant during the night. This is the ultimate tyranny of the minority perpetrated by White males of the Democrat Party, who somehow believe they received a pass and thus, even though white, their holier than Whitey perspectives and attitudes make them appear a little darker every day. But they really kid themselves as they are still as white as newly fallen snow; but their souls are darker and darker and darker for sure.

Chapter 4 Where Did All the Hate Come From?

I LOVE ALL RACES

NO RACE HATE IN MY HEART

makeameme.org

Love is everything God is Love 🖤

Hate for Blacks, Browns, Whites, everybody else

There is a crowd-sourced repository of internet slang that is rife with racist and sexist content and lots of stuff that we should want to keep it from our children. It is known as the Urban Dictionary. Its owner Aaron Peckham doesn't seem to care one bit about the drivel as he smiles all the way to the bank. It's currently the 31st most-visited site in the country, and last month it grabbed nearly 130 million-pageviews.

Clearly some people get their lessons in life from reading alternative sources. We all know the real definition of *White people*, but let's test our understanding with what we would find in the "crowd-sourced racist and sexist Urban Dictionary: "What is the meaning of *White* people?

The top definition from the "people's dictionary," right or wrong is *"Someone who shoots up schools.* Then they show an example:

Guy#1: *Did you hear about that school shooting?*
Guy#2: *It was probably the white people.*

Other definitions include the following "compliments"

#red necks
#jack asses
#crackers
#honkies
#inbred

Well, there you have it. The slang scum on the Internet do not like Whitey!

Where did all the hate come from?

Most would answer with two words: **Left** & **Schools.**

When I grew up, as we discussed in Chapter 3, there was no hate for Blacks or browns or other non-Whites of which I was aware. Not in my neighborhood and not in my schools – St Boniface School or Meyers High School. My college, was so patriotic that in my Freshman year, we even marched in favor of the Vietnam War.

I always felt when such hate began to materialize, or I saw the riots of the 1960's that it was either localized to the big cities or made up. When Barack Obama was elected as the first post racial president, though I did not vote for him, I felt good that this would eliminate any residue of racism that might be left in any part of the USA. I did not protest Obama like the left protests Trump. I looked on the bright side. I instead believed that if he could kill all racism forever, even though he was not a conservative Democrat like me, I would be happy with him. He could have but did not.

Instead, unfortunately, the racial divide which I thought was already gone reappeared in just a few years of Obama. There are those who must have always believed that White people were always supposedly picking on Black people. I did not see it that way then, and I do not see it that way now. There was no more disdain for Blacks as there is for Whites, Reds, or Yellows.

The notion of White privilege was nowhere in sight from my eyes and I was aghast when I heard about the idea for the first time. White privilege is in fact a coordinated response of far-left Democrats who believe that Republicans are comprised of mostly white males who hate women and who hate all other races and subgroupings. That is, it in a nut shell so look no further. It is not true but it is what they preach.

There are historians who suggest that Barack Obama sealed his racial legacy the moment he sealed victory in the 2008 election. It was difficult to imagine that a black man would occupy a White House built by slaves. It was actually history-defying as well as a history-making achievement. It could have been even lots better if the President were able to mask his pro-blackness and his anti-whiteness a little better than he did.

Regarding the White House and slave labor, some find it shocking, but it is true. Construction on the President's House began in 1792 in Washington, D.C., a new capital situated in sparsely settled region far from a major population center. The decision to place the capital on land ceded by two pro-slavery states-Virginia and Maryland-ultimately influenced the acquisition of laborers to construct its public buildings.

The D.C. commissioners, charged by Congress with building the new city under the direction of the president, initially planned to import workers from Europe to meet their new labor needs. However, as they advertised for workers and craftsmen, the response was dismal and soon they decided to turn to African Americans—both enslaved and free—to provide the bulk of labor that built the White House, the United States Capitol, and other early government buildings. It would be nice if the slaves involved were given their freedom, but I have no account of that at least during the construction.

Stonemason Collen Williamson trained the enslaved people on the spot at the government's quarry at Aquia, Virginia. Enslaved people quarried and cut the rough stone that was later dressed and laid by Scottish masons to erect the walls of the President's House. The slaves joined a work force that included local white laborers and artisans from Maryland and Virginia, as well as immigrants from Ireland, Scotland, and other European nations.

Back to the theme...

There were two events early in Obama's residency that I remember that got me thinking that something was not right about a new perspective on Whitism.

1. The Beer Summit
2. Mmm Mmm Mmm Barack Hussein Obama

1. Most who had reached the age of reason still recall that on July 16, 2009, a Black Harvard University "professor" Henry Louis Gates Jr. was arrested at his Cambridge, Massachusetts, home by a local White police officer, Sgt. James Crowley. The officer was responding to a 9-1-1 caller's report of men breaking and entering the residence.

The arrest initiated a series of events that unfolded under the spotlight of the international news media. Most of us still can recall the Beer Summit which was President Obama's way of defusing an issue in which he had jumped the gun on racism. He assumed the White officers had a chip on their shoulder for Black people.

2. In what most Americans saw as an act of political propaganda towards young school children, the country was surprised that the president's Education Department had sent out orders to schools across the nation to sing a song of Obama praise in the public schools. To show how it was received by those with a skeptical eye against propagandizing American youth, towards or against political positions or people, on Friday, September 25, 2009, just three months after the Beer Summit, Michael Steel responded. Steel, then head of the Republican National Committee sent a now viral blast email:

"impressionable youngsters at a public school in New Jersey ... have been instructed to sing the praises of 'Barack Hussein Obama.'"

It could have been misinterpreted but few objective minds thought so. For many who know history, it brought back memories of the Hitler Youth Movement and all the propaganda directed at the youth in the years before WWII. For those who are not on the inside, it had elements in it that were frightening.

The reason many Americans were alarmed at the days when *Mmm Mm Mmm* was the song of the day, consider another day and another time of such propaganda.

From the 1920s onwards, the Nazi Party targeted German youth as a special audience for its propaganda messages. These messages emphasized that the Party was a movement of youth: dynamic, resilient, forward-looking, and hopeful. Millions of German young people were won over to Nazism in the classroom and through extracurricular activities. In January 1933, the Hitler Youth had only 50,000 members, but by the end of the year this figure had increased to more than 2 million. It was not by accident. Hitler was training his armies. By 1936, membership in the Hitler Youth increased to 5.4 million before it became mandatory in 1939.

"These boys and girls enter our organizations [at] ten years of age, and often for the first time get a little fresh air; after four years of the Young Folk they go on to the Hitler Youth, where we have them for another four years . . . And even if they are still not complete National Socialists, they go to Labor Service and are smoothed out there for another six, seven months . . . And whatever class consciousness or social status might still be left . . . the Wehrmacht [German armed forces] will take care of that."
—*Adolf Hitler (1938)*

Can you understand the chill many felt?

Nonetheless Obama's Department of Education put out this drivel and there were so many Obama advocates in the teaching profession that love him without reservation that it was introduced to the children. Fox News printed the words to two *Hail Obama* songs: How does this work on the smell test with you?

Song 1:
Mm, mmm, mm!
Barack Hussein Obama

He said that all must lend a hand
To make this country strong again
Mmm, mmm, mm!
Barack Hussein Obama

He said we must be fair today
Equal work means equal pay
Mmm, mmm, mm!
Barack Hussein Obama

He said that we must take a stand
To make sure everyone gets a chance
Mmm, mmm, mm!
Barack Hussein Obama

He said red, yellow, black or white
All are equal in his sight
Mmm, mmm, mm!
Barack Hussein Obama
Yes!
Mmm, mmm, mm
Barack Hussein Obama

Song 2:
Hello, Mr. President we honor you today!
For all your great accomplishments, we all doth say "hooray!"

Hooray, Mr. President! You're number one!
The first black American to lead this great nation!

Hooray, Mr. President we honor your great plans
To make this country's economy number one again!

Hooray Mr. President, we're really proud of you!
And we stand for all Americans under the great Red, White, and Blue!

So continue ---- Mr. President we know you'll do the trick
So here's a hearty hip-hooray ----

Hip, hip hooray!
Hip, hip hooray!
Hip, hip hooray!

Kinda gets to you doesn't it... just like this old Führer favorite from
Germany reproduced below:

In Praise of the Führer

We often heard the sound of your voice
And listened silently, with folded hands,
As each word sank into our souls.
We all know: The day will come
That frees us from need and compulsion.

What is a year!
What is a law that would restrain us —
The pure faith that you have given us
Pulses through, guides our young lives.
My Führer, you alone are the way, the goal!

And that, ladies and gentlemen is the music show for today.

Is hating white Guys the new norm for Schools??

The ditties in this section give a perspective about how far it went
wrong. How Whitey became the target for many far leftists hoping
they can make the rest of America feel the same.

I have no idea who Lee Siegel is but just today I read he was in
horror about Mitt Romney being so egregiously White. Like many
reading this book right now, I did not know until recently that being
white was a sin. If I had known this when I was learning all about
being Catholic in Grade School at St. Boniface, I would have
confessed it after Novena on some Monday afternoon before playing
after-school sockball with my classmates. It would have been a softie

sin that I could have slipped in during Confession after telling the Priest about the big ones such as stealing a quarter from my father's pants pocket when he was sleeping.

When I found out that Romney's whiteness was perceived to be a bad thing, I continued to search, and I found that his whole family is White; and worse than that; he has a lot of children. Moreover, the family is rich, and they are all good looking. This is surely a veritable nightmare for a card-carrying member of the hostile anti-white elite, however else they may be known. Perhaps if the Romneys all starred in a Hollywood scum film, they would be OK being white

Back when Romney was preparing to beat Barack "Mmm Mm Mmm" Obama out for president of the US, The NY Times was dyeing the Grey Lady's hair to make the Times look whiter to Whites. At the time, the real bad guys were worried that Romney might choose a Latino VP candidate (who they supposed would be Marco Rubio). Of course, this recent neoconservative would have had to change his tune on immigration but with a non-white on the ticket, Romney theoretically according to the racists, would have had a better chance than with white as snow, Paul Ryan.

But, even with a black or Hispanic VEEP, the word at the DNC was that "Romney is just sooooo white. Why, he is even whiter than the Osmonds." He could not get elected in Democratic Elitist America with or without Rubio because he did not look like any member of the Jackson Five or a recent immigrant from South of the Border. Perhaps if the press found that he was a blood relative of Al Sharpton it might have helped.

The hatred of the leftist Democrat Elite and the progressive socialists for White people is palpable. You can feel it in your bones. The media is full of people who subscribe to a message of hate, hate, and more hate. And, since they have the supposed power to declare Whitey, bad, Whitey must be bad. I say: "No way!"

A guy named Harold Meyerson wrote in The Washington Bleep in 2008 that the Republicans now more than ever are the White Folks' Party. They are the nasty party of the American past. Myerson forgot conveniently that Lincoln was the first Republican President and that the Democrats were the founders and the first members of the Ku Klux Clan. Oh yes—it is true.

In fact, American Blacks would be outraged if the corrupt and dishonest fake-news press ever admitted that they have the real facts from history.com. They can find them if they want. I am talking about the fact that in Pulaski, Tennessee, a group of Confederate veterans convened on December 24, 1865 six months after the Civil War ended on May 13. They formed a top-secret society that they christened the "Ku Klux Klan." The KKK was founded in many ways to be the military arm of the Democratic Party.

Prominent Democrats, annoyed at slavery being outlawed for good, were active in the Klan from the time of its inception. They did not want to admit their roles however. So, in recent years, with the help of a complicity lying press, they have done their best to blame Republicans for their own culpability in slavery. Many Americans, both black and white from the left side of the plate have accepted this major piece of fake news as true.

The KKK rapidly grew from a secret social fraternity to a paramilitary force bent on reversing the federal government's progressive Reconstruction Era-activities in the South, especially policies that elevated the rights of the local African American population.

The name of the Ku Klux Klan was derived from the Greek word kyklos, meaning "circle," and the Scottish-Gaelic word "clan," which was probably chosen for the sake of alliteration. Under a platform of philosophized white racial superiority, the group employed violence as a means of pushing back Reconstruction and its enfranchisement of African Americans. Former Confederate General Nathan Bedford Forrest was the KKK's first grand wizard; in 1869, he unsuccessfully tried to disband it after he grew critical of the Klan's excessive violence.

Most prominent in counties where the races were relatively balanced, the KKK engaged in terrorist raids against African Americans and white Republicans at night, employing intimidation, destruction of property, assault, and murder to achieve its aims and influence upcoming elections. The Klan hated the white Republicans who beat them in the Civil War.

Republicans were repulsed by the Klan and still are today. Lying Democrats who created the Klan continue to attempt to persuade the people that when you think Klan and White Superiority, it is a Republican theme. Not so!

In fact, in a number of Southern states, Republicans organized militia units to break up the Klan. In 1871, the Ku Klux Act passed Congress, authorizing President Ulysses S. Grant to use military force to suppress the KKK. The Ku Klux Act resulted in nine South Carolina counties being placed under martial law and thousands of arrests.

In 1882, the U.S. Supreme Court declared the Ku Klux Act unconstitutional, but by that time Reconstruction had ended, the KKK had mostly faded away.

The 20th century witnessed two revivals of the KKK: one in response to immigration in the 1910s and '20s, and another in response to the African American civil rights movement of the 1950s and '60s. So much time has passed that Democrats have successfully posited the untruth in the media that Republicans were responsible for the KKK atrocities. White Republicans did their best to stop the KKK and today's Blacks still have not thanked them.

The Whites, Blacks, and others in the Democratic Party, in league with the corrupt press / fake news media enjoy picking on Republicans with the power of the Fourth Estate. They equate white males to Republicans, so they can use the term "Whites" and have it mean Republicans to many. Yet, here I am a JFK Democrat, of all-Irish heritage and yes, folks, I am white and proud of it.

Recently, since they do not see many of the Blacks or other non-Whites in the Republican Party, they have begun to focus their attention on white males. The title of this book is White People are Bad! Bad! Bad! As silly as that is, the elite Democrats and the corrupt press are doing their best to convince America that it is so, And, as you know they do not mind lying to make their point.

A nice shot fired at Republicans by Democratic in prose for example, would be something such as this: "Republican conventions have long been bastions of de facto Caucasian exclusivity... , but coming right after the diversity of the [Democratic Convention in Denver], this year's GOP convention is almost shockingly — un-Americanly — White. Long term, this whiteness is a huge problem." Who says? The problem is any focus on color instead of the issues.

Donald Trump, for example in 2018, a candidate who once asked potential Black voters, "What do you have to lose?" brought Black unemployment to the lowest ever in just 18 months in office. Trump has been rewarded by polls, which once placed him at 15% black favorability, and now they clock him in at a brisk 30%. So, perhaps the Blacks, who before voters found out their stance on the KKK were once owned by the Democratic Party have decided on their own not to be slaves to the Democratic luddites anymore.

I do not know who wrote the following but it sure sounds like stuff that I have penned in my day:

"The hatred we now see in the mainstream media was of course prefigured by anti-White intellectuals, writing in rarified academic settings or little literary magazines."

Susan Sontag's famous line that "the white race is the cancer of human history" first appeared in The Partisan Review, the flagship journal of the elite New York Intellectuals, in 1967. Or it could have been Freud and the Frankfurt School. Who knows? The only thing well known in 2018 is that Whitey, who once was called a dirty Republican is not looked upon as cute any more.

What has begun to frighten me and my lily-white exterior a bit recently and there are those who think every Whitey should be spooked, is that the hostility toward Whites is mainstream among the non-White constituencies of the hostile elite—Blacks and Latinos in particular. They do not mind firing literary Molotov cocktails at Whites, especially White males, and when they gather in a group they are often well armed with real Molotov cocktails and they don't seem to care what they steal and who gets hurt.

"Mmm Mmm Mmm" may have been bad but as time has passed, it has gotten worse for Whites and Trump's whiteness seems to make him the last guy anybody would pick to help all the White males out there who are forced to put up with this ridiculousness every day.

Chapter 5 Off the Wall Groups and Schools

The stories of groups and schools going off the wall against Whites are more and more commonplace. Just recently there are two reports where school officials have explicitly condoned anti-White attitudes and, in the case of the Kansas City school system, even anti-White behavior. With Whites making up 60% of the documented population today, one thing is for sure. Whites have the numbers still and do not have to take this pounding every day. One problem of course is that Democrat white males line up with non-Whites against Whites. I don't understand it, but I see it just like you do.

There was an article in "The American Thinker" titled _Was Boy in K.C. Fire Attack a Victim of His School's Racist Teaching?_ "), Selwyn Duke, a traditionalist media personality whose work has been published widely online and in print, appearing at outlets such as The Hill, has shown that the Kansas City school system tolerates teachers who encourage harassment of White students and who provide a constant stream of anti-White propaganda in their classes. No harassment is the right amount and so this could not be tolerated.

These attacks occurred at a school in which 13-year-old Allen Coon was subjected to "a vicious physical racial attack. Two older black teens doused him with gasoline and set him alight, saying, this is what you deserve'. You get what you deserve, white boy.'"
The two-headed Allen looks like "the classic all-American white boy," says his mother, and "after the first week of school he was nothing but racially harassed." She says that "he was called every racial slur you can imagine," such as "honkey," "cracker," "Whitey," and "guero" (a Spanish slang term for Whites that can be used in a derogatory way).

He was, she reports, pushed into lockers and was jumped in the bathroom. And even before the recent attack, he was sometimes menaced by groups that would follow him part of the way home. More damning, even than that though, is that multiple adult educators of the school were complicit in the harassment. Mrs. Coon is saddened and outraged as we all would be. She related another incident in which a teacher known as Ms. Carla Kinder called Allen "Casper" and then "got all the students to get involved." There were other times the students would initiate the harassment, and the teachers would pick up the baton. "They would tease him; people would make fun of him, and they'd chime in," said Coon.

Of course, there was a media blackout of the explicitly racial assault against Coon which occurred around the same time as the wall-to-wall coverage of the Trayvon Martin shooting where the attempt by the media and Black activists to portray Martin as an innocent victim of a racially motivated killer. That story as we know got more and more ridiculous the more we learned about Martin and Zimmerman.

While Kansas City takes no action and in fact tolerates Black teachers spewing hatred toward Whites, it's not the only place and not the only race. The Los Angeles school system encourages Latino hatred toward Whites. It helps to be reminded that white is no longer the dominant racial makeup in California. In as recent as 2015, California had the largest minority population in the United States. Non-Hispanic Whites decreased from about 76.3 - 78% of the state's population in 1970 to 38.0% in 2015. While the population of minorities accounts for 100.7 million of 300 million U.S. residents, 20% of the national total live in California

Mary Morrison is a pen name for a person fearful of having opinion attributed to her. Since I do not know her real name, I cannot nor, would I give her up. She penned an article for American Renaissance, which is on ground zero with the failed educational system. The title of the piece is "White Teacher in an LA School". The system where she works permits students to come to school with iPods and iPhones, but no books, no paper and no pencils. It's a system where teachers, not administrators, administrative policies, or students are blamed for the failures of their low-IQ, low-achieving students:

"And what is needed? More teacher oversight, more professional development, better, newer methods of teaching, and textbooks loaded with photos that reflect "changing demographics" so 'students of color' can see 'others who look like them.'" Right.

Back to the main point of this reference. This system for all its flaws is also quite tolerant of hatred toward Whites. Eliminating Ethnic studies such as Mexican Contributions to the US has been used as a tool by some districts to take the "rah rah" out of the "game." Places such as Tucson which are 60% minority would be happy to have all teaching in Spanish and let the white kids figure out how to learn.

There are some obvious no-no's where there are racial tensions among students. For example, Students at East LA's Roosevelt High School enter the school by walking by a 400-foot mural "depicting Europeans hanging and burning Mexicans, smashing their babies' heads against rocks, and feeding the flesh of Mexicans to their 'war dogs.'" That is enough to get quiet students flamed up.

The media does not report the news; it takes sides. For example, the anti-White LA Times is quite happy with such depictions (while ignoring Latino ethnic cleansing of Blacks from many areas of Los Angeles), noting that the mural "'presents a colorful depiction of the rape, slaughter and enslavement of North America's indigenous people by genocidal Europeans.' Thank you for your help Dear Fourth Estate.

When the board of trustees of the Los Angeles Unified School District was asked whether it thought that this was an appropriate sentiment for high school students, its official response was that the mural 'merely presents a different perspective' and that there was 'no intent to remove it.'" If the objective is to agitate minority students so that they harass and attack Whites, would it not be even more effective if the District hired a professional artist and overpainted the faces on the mural with pictures of specific local minority student's mothers and fathers

Close your eyes in today's upside-down world and imagine the District's response to a mural with messages promoting the achievements of Whites and the legitimacy of having a sense of White identity and interests. How long would that stay up. It is a different perspective, right?

Is this harassment at peak or is this just the beginning of the future of White victimization as Whites move from being a clear majority in the US to a minority? However bad it is now, it will be vastly worse in the future. When there are officially condoned anti-White propaganda and actions at a time when Whites are still almost 2/3 of the population, imagine what it will be like when Whites are less than half. The date is now set for 2045 for the white population to become a minority. What then?

The newest census population projections confirm the importance of racial minorities as the primary demographic engine of the nation's future growth, countering an aging, slow-growing and soon to be declining white population. The new statistics project that the nation will become "minority white" in 2045. During that year, Whites will comprise 49.9 percent of the population in contrast to 24.6 percent for Hispanics, 13.1 percent for Blacks, 7.8 percent for Asians, and 3.8 percent for multiracial populations.

Besides continuing illegal immigration, the shift is the result of two trends. First, between 2018 and 2060, gains will continue in the combined racial minority populations, growing by 74 percent. Second, during this time frame, the aging white population will see a modest immediate gain through 2023, and then experience a long-term decline through 2060, a consequence of more deaths than births.

Think about what it will be for you and your family when you become a minority and the former minorities have been trained in the schools to treat you with hostility.

The hostile and dishonest elites who control the media already condone government-facilitated anti-White hatred. You can project how things will be in the future without major scientific tools just by looking at the recent past. They will be increasingly powerful as their constituents become an ever-larger component of the population. Suckup Whiteys, if I may be so crass, are typically from well-to-do hoity-toity historical families. They are major supporters of what can best be termed a facade of official multicultural utopianism. It is so great to support people not like me. Humph! Really!

There is a notion that was first promoted by Horace Kallen, which represents the bedrock attitude of the organized Jewish community since World War II. In it, the future is depicted as a glorious harmony of races, all working together in pursuit of moral perfection. How long can such a notion last?

It seems the gloves are already coming off though open discussion has not erupted yet. However, it is clearer every day that beneath the faux utopian optimism there is a real hatred that will ultimately endanger all Whites. Those who most effusively promote utopian multiracial harmony as studied, are those with the fiercest racial hatreds.

It has been characterized as if millions of Whites are walking zombie-like into this future, with no mainstream political option that will do anything to save them. What might we do? We can see that the mere Whiteness of a gentle soul such as Mitt Romney's may be more than enough to trigger the naïve hatred that too many have toward Whites. But Romney even if he were elected in 2012, would do nothing to alter the situation. What could he do?

When I was the director of advanced technology implementation for Misericordia University, there was a big push towards the notion of diversity on campus. The term was not well oiled at the time and so there were those who thought it meant ethnicity, but it was more than that. There were also those who felt it was a trick word so that

Homosexuals, Lesbians, people with AIDS, and any LGBT Gay could be declared normal. There were a lot of suspicions regarding the word diversity itself. Misericordia University was so concerned that people understood the meaning as the institution intended and so they appointed a Director of Diversity to help make sure the right message got out.

No matter where you go, the word is often used when talking about the presence of people on a campus who differ in terms of race, culture, ethnicity, religion, socioeconomic status, sexual orientation, and ability. It also means the presence of people with diverse opinions, political views, and academic passions. However, a true, comprehensive definition of diversity should also include ways in which a diverse population engages with and explores its differences.

The irony is that as most campuses today are havens for liberal progressives and socialists/communists, the end game for this community is far-left radical group thinking with little to no diversity. Free speech has become such an endangered capability on so many campuses, the administrations have cordoned off small areas called free speech zones ; as the default for the campus community is *no free speech*. However, all the speech one wants if it comes from the bible of the left is permissible.

Consequently, we may say with conviction today that for all the talk, it does not really constitute progress on campus when the proponents of diversity are the proponents of groupthink and they resort to the behavior that was once previously the preserve of sexists and racists? And for good measure, we can throw in the fact, that the news reporters / creators are preaching the new fake news saying that most white people are bad," Bull!

Did all of this come from diversity? Probably not but something evolved to where we are today in America in 2018 and it is not good

Mush minds

Students come to college with mush heads ready to absorb all the good (and the bad) that is given them. Today they get groupthink diversity propaganda and it is not good for students or for their future lives as loyal patriotic Americans. Along the way, these young people are exposed to a variety of new and yes, diverse political ideas.

In an ideal world or say a world such as one not much different from one fifty years ago, students would be challenged to rethink their beliefs to gain a perspective they may not have known even existed. Unfortunately, on college campuses, in recent years, students have become more susceptible to liberal progressive Democratic groupthink for a variety of reasons surrounding a fear of offending someone or becoming part of a minority opinion.

Today, campus groupthink says that white folk are racists and white students need remedial training so that they are prepared to see their whiteness as a bad thing. It is not only groupthink; some universities even have courses to get white students to renounce their whiteness. Why? Because it is obviously bad. Try a course titled: Dismantling White Privilege, Power, and Supremacy .

Where does this take us? Should white folk, 62% so far and declining in the US, acquiesce to the hate mongers and say they are right? We are just bad! bad! bad! I don't think so. Just like Blacks cannot accept a premise that as a race, they are bad, neither can Whites. Just like Blacks must fight, Whites must fight.

Living in Wilkes-Barre, PA all my life, I was unaware that it was OK to single out any race as being better or worse than any other. Yet, it is not only permissible on college campuses, they the administration takes sides. And, today they act like the debate is over and Whites are the problem in America. I am not buying it, nor are most other Whites that I know who are not hard and fast lefties.

Jews News interpreted a speech my First Lady Michelle Obama as racist. That's how they saw it, but their interpretation has not been accepted by the leftist fact-finders. So, the fact finders talk about a false rumor claiming First Lady Michelle Obama had stated that "white folks are what's wrong with America" during a speech at Tuskegee University started recirculating online in November 2015 after the web site Jews News repurposed an article from May of the same year.

Who knows what she meant? She is not thankful for her eight years in office with her husband and It comes out often in her speeches and interviews. "Knowing that after eight years of working really hard for this country, there are still people who won't see me for what I am because of my skin color," she told one crowd. But she does not say who? Who knows but it a white person said what she said, there would be PR hell to pay.

The point, of course is that white is not bad nor is black or other colors as I try to explain this phenomenon of color classification and judgment by color. It is ridiculous. Quite a lot of people of all skin colors are bad, but probably not a majority of those people—not even close. Most people want to be good, but they are in various ways weak. And a few people are brave.

Yet across America, we have campuses in which faculty of color, women and particularly those scholars who are outspoken about dismantling the master narratives of white supremacy within our colleges and universities comment in the negative about a White America founded of, by and for whites. They believe Whites are bad because they took the time and the risks of life and limb to found America as its own independent country and today. Today , these faculty members have declared America bad because its founders were White. Who knows who founded Africa as a continent but it was not Whitey and yet these same racist faculty members stay in America when they can get the relief they seem to seek in Africa.

As an aside, if you ask the Internet Who founded Africa, you get: "Jan van Riebeeck founded Cape Town in 1652, starting the European exploration and colonization of South Africa." But, we know that for most South Africans, Nelson Mandela is the father of their nation - many even called him "Tata", a Xhosa word for father. It was sometimes forgotten that he was also a real father of six, grandfather of 18, great-grandfather of eight, and husband to three women.

Africa is a huge country, mostly black, regardless of who gets credit for founding it. American Academics who smugly contest the legitimacy of America's founding do have a choice. The Whites after

1492 in shiploads after shiploads from Europe had a choice also –
stay in America or try to get back to the Europe. We all have choices
without ripping at the choices of others.

Many over the years after gaining freedom after the Civil War, have
conceptualized it and dreamed about returning to the "Mama
Africa." There was a "Back to Africa" movement in the 1920s in
which Marcus Garvey suggested that that African Americans could
only attain social equality by moving back to Africa, and he saw the
continent as the only place in which self-emancipation could be
attained.

Others thought Garvey was all wet as the African Continent was
anything but peaceful. They countered that the idea of sending an
oppressed group of people to find equality in a place where the
individuals to whom the land belong face systematic oppression (by
way of colonialism) doesn't make much sense and could only exist in
the realm of idealism and romanticism.
Some African Americans nonetheless, and Utopia may have its only
existence in Academia, have constructed for themselves a Utopia
image of Africa. Some say that the afrocentric rhetoric with which
some discuss the continent often conceptualizes a glorified heritage
even if it was never glorious. Such rhetoric romanticizes Africa,
likening the continent to a sort of unblemished and innocent woman,
"Mama Africa" is the name they give. But they stay in America
because what you have is often better than what is on the other side
of the fence.

We have learned that courage is not color specific and it is not
gender-specific, either. My wife is tough as nails and sweet as pie.
She may not be the bravest person I know, but she is as close as it
gets. All through history, men supposedly had a role as major
breadwinner and protector, yet there is no doubt there are women
who are stronger and braver than men. Some say when manliness is
exhibited, it is more like "confidence in a situation of risk."
Nonetheless, there are many, especially feminists who would argue
that manliness is bad! bad! bad! And it is the essence of that evil that
good women (feminists in particular) are eradicating.

The point again is that it is that somehow it is OK for Blacks and Yellows and Reds to find Whites offensive and the press seems overjoyed by the "from anywhere" attacks on Whitey. Nonetheless, it is not OK for Whites, the supposed major perpetrators of injustice in all mankind, to find Blacks, Yellows, or Reds offensive.

Well, this may be news for some but other than hollow-brain leftist Whites, the majority of Whites do not accept that premise. Whites may very well find Blacks, Yellows, and Reds offensive and this inner feeling cannot be legislated away. Reds may find Yellows offensive; Yellows, Blacks, etc. etc.

Nobody can legislate how one entity should feel against another. And, so the premise behind a course such as *Dismantling White Privilege, Power, and Supremacy* is not going to cut it very long in any environment other than with academic elites (coffee breath professors). But it does show how far group-think and diversity can cloud otherwise good minds.

Chapter 6 Is Donald Trump White?

Trump the Nationalist / Populist chose to run as a Republican

We all know the leftist Democrats knew that Mitt Romney was soooo white, he had to be a loser. He was a real Republican unlike Donald Trump who like many voters chooses the Republican side because the leftist progressive Democrats are so bad, somebody has got to stop them.

I am a registered Democrat in the order of JFK. I did not leave the Party, it left me. I ran for office a number of times, but few Democrats like me because I will never bow to the altar of Pelosi and Schumer. But as a reluctant Democrat, a JFK Democrat for sure. I am brazen enough to say that I can't stand either of the Party's Congressional Leaders.

I suspect with all the white males in the Democrat Party, that there are many like me who wish the Democrat leadership would bring out the old playbooks from when our parents became voters. The old playbooks were pro-American citizen oriented and the Democrats thought about helping the regular people, not just the fringe elements and illegal aliens.

Most know from all the great Trumpian stories out there that one of the main reasons Donald Trump won the Republican nomination in 2016 was his commitment to the populist and nationalist agenda. He planned on day one to put the people of American first, way ahead of the special interests and other countries. These emphases, in addition to his brash television persona, and his likeable demeanor enabled him to stand above the crowded GOP field and grab the nomination from great candidates like Ted Cruz and Marco Rubio.

A sure indication of Mr. Trump's populist-nationalism was his commitment to taxes on imported goods, or tariffs, intended to protect vulnerable American industries. And just a few months ago, he made good on his campaign pledge by proposing new levies on imported steel and aluminum. In recent weeks, the economy is showing more life. Though some people have issues with tariffs. I believe they are good for America as I have written two books in this regard, *Tariffs Are Good for America !!!* and *Saving America*. Both can be accessed via Amazon at amazon.com/author/brianwkelly

What is a Leftist?

Before we continue with this chapter, let's look at a list of Mark Levin's thirteen points which differentiate Leftists from conservatives. I will not have to change a word as the "We" in this short list is US.

1. We believe in the Constitution, they believe in centralism.
2. We believe in individualism, they believe in conformity.
3. We believe in private property, they believe in collectivism.
4. We believe in prosperity, they believe in redistribution.
5. We believe in separation of powers, they believe in the administrative state.
6. We believe in eternal truths, they believe in ideological social engineering.
7. We believe in cultural stability, they believe in constant transformation.
8. We believe in real science, they believe in social science.
9. We believe in the rights of man, they believe in the power of government.
10. We believe in the moral order, they believe in situational ethics.
11. We believe in liberty, they believe in a growing authoritarianism.

12. We believe in education, they believe in indoctrination.
13. We believe in civil society, they believe in the federal leviathan

The current Party leaders seem to pay homage to all non-whites, legal and illegal—it does not matter. The Democrat Party lets its White male American constituency rot without a job to be had.

Embarrassed that Trump clearly favors Americans over illegal interlopers, the illegal interloper-loving Democrats have been telling their constituency that having a job is not as important as being a loyal Democrat. They add that the latest Queen of Mean, Nancy Pelosi would be happy to take all those Trump crumbs from the tax cut away from all Democrats because she believes nobody a thousand dollars in crumbs. This would show Republicans that they can shove their tax cuts….even if it means a few less loaves of bread to the loyal Democrat constituency. She and Chuck Schumer believe in Party over people.

Is it possible that Donald Trump alone is the reason for the backlash against white males? Who cares if it is? It is the worst of fake news from the NY Times! It is a leftist, corrupt media-driven backlash signifying nothing but another take-down strategy of the progressive left to remove a duly elected president of the US. I am glad that they do not own the US Constitution, or we might have to worry.

With the NY Times picking up an avowed anti-white activist and mud slinger v Whites claiming it is OK because she is yellow, we know that no support for any Whitey is coming soon from the NY Times. The old Grey Lady ain't what she used to be!

I have read that l'affaire Jeong has taught us at least one thing, it's that the people who claim most vociferously to be anti-racist are nothing of the sort. On the contrary, race is all there is for them. They are sickly obsessed with race, seeing almost everything through the prism of ethnicity.

They are as worthless as their worth description of white males, red males, yellow females or whatever they may bring to the fore. They're in favor of categorizing people according to racial criteria. What they object to is not racial discrimination, but racial discrimination against the wrong groups. They believe that discriminating against Whites of any religion or sex is OK as long as their ideology is on the right side of center and they support the Democrat Party.

Sarah Jeong is an activist posing as a journalist and the NY Times accepted the ruse to make news instead of reporting it as their charter suggests. Yes, the Grey Lady admits bringing Jeong in on August 1, 2018 as an editorial writer and as a member of their editorial board even though they know she is a racist who flaunts her negativism via caustic quick tweets.

Of course, the Times vetted her social media history, poring over it with great care (or, as Donald Trump might put it, "poured over"). Some pungent Tweets showed up that show her character, but none moved the Times out of their original hiring proposition.

Those tweets of Jeong's that have attracted the most attention are the straightforwardly racist ones — "white people are bullshit," "#CancelWhitePeople," and so on — though, to my mind, her assertion that free speech is a conservative dog whistle is far more alarming for a journalist than any of these.

Of course, with the Times as an advocate of regulated v free speech, it is easy to see their favor with Jeong. We'll all have to contend with her claptrap, but we do not have to buy in, like, or respect her or the Times for it. If the Grey Lady was ever a great symbol and a news organization to emulate, those days are gone.

And so, as we ponder whether Jeong is a response to Trump because white people like Trump because he is White, we do know that the dishonest NY Times does not care. Their sole objective is to make the President look bad if they can, hoping their case is enough to force Trump out of office. Yes, if they, by hook or by crook, they can make fun of Donald Trump and have everybody think he is worthless, they feel they picked up some ground. They think it is a KO punch to whack the "undeserving" President by calling him "white." How ridiculous.

What the far left forgets, because the Third Reich never permitted dissent, is that the people, less and less readers of the NY Times, still have a voice in America. Those of us who elected Trump as President are still making noise. Some of the noise comes in the form of poetry and some in the form of songs .

I am pleased to show an example of that noise that came in my email just today. It is a song made into a poem or a poem made into a song. It is not about BIG John, but it sounds that way because it is about BIG Don. Donald J. Trump, a mountain of a man in spirit. And, it does not wax to be political. Here it is. The YouTube link comes after the words.

Big Don – A Mountain of a President

Big Don

Big Don

Every Sunday night at nine, on tv he'll arrive
With his hair, he's tall, might exceed two forty-five
Not a billionaire bolder, proud and pouty of lips
And everybody knows, nobody pops bird flips to Big Don

Big Don, Big Don, Big Bad Don, (Big Don)

"Celebrity Apprentice" Don calls home
He's the King of New York town, just ask him, it's shown
He doesn't smile much, gets smirky like Captain Bligh
Say something wrong, you'll see that evil eye from Big Don

This season on the show, he has All Stars
Past players claw and fight in the boardroom wars
Guys like Rodman's flair, with a huge right hand
Sent that big ol' drink a water back to Dribble Land, did Don

Big Don, Big Don, Big Bad Don, (Big Don)

A few hot babes get their bottoms swingin' fine

Some guys half-cracked, the Gary Busey kind
Singers, and actors, lotta' has-beens cast
And each week, one will learn that this'll be their last,
With Don.

Through mistrust, mirrored smoke, of this man made hell
Walks a tyrant of a man, Sunday "Niners" know well
Struts with swag and glimmer, self, he'd love to clone
If it was all his own way, he'd do the whole show alone, Big Don,

Big Don, Big Don, Big Bad Don, (Big Don)

Old Piers Morgan's been there, to number one, he'd shove
And Joan Rivers has won, tough plastic, she's made of
The weak willed may crumble, but the strong don't cave
In order to win, you must be a knave, like Don..

Shore up those timbers, and never back down
Make boardroom rumble, clamp feet, and dig ground
Hunker down, kick ass - watch back, all the time
Screw everyone else, and then just suck up and shine, to Big Don

Big Don, Big Don, Big Bad Don, (Big Don)

Fin'lly scratched Omarosa, fun evil witch
Well, Lil John, he got her canned, with good rap pitch
All her pride just trickled down like sand,
When "You're fired!" was the line - from the big, big man, Big Don

Big Don, Big Don, Big Bad Don, (Big Don)

(Big Don)

Big Bad Don

Hear it on You Tube

https://www.youtube.com/watch?v=w7I_y5qCUPc&feature=youtu
.be

Donald J. Trump
✔ @realDonaldTrump

Is Trump racist?

Wow, what a loaded question. According to more and more
psychologists, everybody is a racist – some a little bit and some a lot.

Some, but few. are explicitly racist while more than we would like to
admit according to the best psychologists that money can buy, many
are implicitly racist by things such as preferring Blacks over Whites
or vice versa. Well, the reality is that if everybody is racist then it
cannot be an egregious sin then!-- Can it be?

One of the proofs put out by those in control of the racist label that
Donald Trump is an explicit racist is his position on the NFL. Some
say he is racist because he tried to own an NFL team a while back
and the NFL would not admit him into the owner's club. Since all
the owners are white, how can that make Trump racist, even if he
holds a grudge against the owners for poor personal treatment?

The NFL is losing fans and money over this fight. So, they finally
created a policy. The NFL's newly enacted policy from May 23
required players to stand for the national anthem or wait in the locker
room. Apparently, the players were outraged at the thought that they
obey management's orders and they showed in the first pre-game
game that they do not respect team or league management.

In May, the league sought to finally end the fan backlash to the
kneeling protests against racial injustice that dominated coverage for

the past two seasons. Now because the players association complained, the NFL will put the anthem rule on hold again after a fresh round of criticism before the preseason began.

Donald Trump picked this issue again knowing that it is an issue which most black players support and the President has basically said what they are doing is bad! bad! bad!. Of course, he never said they were bad… just what they are doing.

The latest round came after the opening games of the NFL preseason on Thursday, August 9. Our President, defending the importance of the US Flag and the country for which it stands, blasted NFL players who took a knee in protest during preseason games, saying that players who fail to stand during the national anthem should be "suspended without pay."

The president's latest broadside against NFL players who kneel during the national anthem came in a tweet the next Friday morning in response to Thursday night's games.

"The NFL players are at it again - taking a knee when they should be standing proudly for the National Anthem. Numerous players, from different teams, wanted to show their "outrage" at something that most of them are unable to define. They make a fortune doing what they love…………," Trump stated.

Trump continued that players should "Be happy, be cool! A football game, that fans are paying soooo much money to watch and enjoy, is no place to protest. Most of that money goes to the players anyway. Find another way to protest. Stand proudly for your National Anthem or be Suspended Without Pay!"

8:32 AM - Aug 10, 2018

This all began with Colin Kaepernick: "I am not going to stand up to show pride in a flag for a country that oppresses black people, and people of color," Kaepernick said in a press conference after first sitting out during the anthem. "To me, this is bigger than football, and it would be selfish on my part to look the other way. There are bodies in the street, and people getting paid leave, and getting away with murder."

He eventually got a lot of support from NFL players but very little support from NFL fans, the fans that pay the huge salaries of NFL players.

Donald Trump, the "White" President of the United States does not like anybody trashing the idea of America, whether they are big shot NFL players or not. There are many ways to protest even at a football game but why cast aspersions on the United States?

It was not long after Kaepernick's protest that on behalf of many Americans, Mr. Trump became a catalyst for the protest in September when he said during a campaign rally in Alabama that he wished that NFL players would be fired for kneeling during the national anthem. Trump made his thoughts well known and I would suggest that most Americans support his position. We know this by looking at the empty seats and the TV ratings of NFL games as well as those suggesting colleges begin to play football on Sundays.

Trump minced no words: "Wouldn't you love to see one of these NFL owners, when somebody disrespects our flag, to say, 'Get that son of a b**** off the field right now, out, he's fired. He's fired,'" Mr. Trump said. "You know, some owner is going to do that. He's going to say, 'That guy that disrespects our flag, he's fired.' And that owner, they don't know it [but] they'll be the most popular person in this country." Yes, I think Trump is right on this one. This should not be a black v white issue it is respect v no respect.

I have yet to see that this protest has denigrated into a race war about football. We have all heard the disgust on both sides of the issue. The fact is this is a fight that did not have to be as the player millionaires could sponsor a rally every week on their time, not fans time. If they chose to highlight their cause, no matter what the cause – racism, police violence, free speech, or not showing patriotism.

There are many regular joes across the nation that care much more about America than a bunch of millionaire football players, who have many other ways at their disposal to make their collective points.

On the extreme perhaps, I have a number of acquaintances who will not watch another NFL game. Some have suggested this is another opportunity time for businessmen who have been shot out of having an NFL team to begin their own league.

There are many who think football has become a black sport I have heard a recommendation that since 70% of the players are black, and this problem began as a black issue and it continues because it is definitely a black issue, why not create two leagues, a White Football League and a Black Football League. It would be interesting to see if fans went with their own race or with the better league which would probably be the Black League. Can you imagine the excitement if there were ever a Super Bowl between the leagues?

If there were no Whites in the BFL, would there still be anthem protests? Would there be anthem protests in the WFL? Maybe if nothing else the formation of two additional leagues for teams that played on Tuesday and Wednesday nights, would give a lot of additional players, White and Black an opportunity to excel in sports.

Rush Limbaugh thinks he found a great suggestion to solve the NFL Players Anthem Protest if it really is about racial injustice. Here is the caller's suggestion from the Rush Limbaugh Show:

> RUSH: I was reading an NFL website. Doesn't matter what it is. I read a comment from a reader of this website about the ongoing controversy the NFL is having over what to do about the national anthem and the players taking a knee. And, you know, there is a massive boycott for the NFL games planned on Veterans Day, November 12th. Have you heard about this?
>
> A bunch of fans are trying to organize a massive boycott of the NFL on that one day. I don't know how successful they're going to be, but it's all rooted in the fact that they are protesting the flag and protesting the military when they are rich beyond most people's wildest imaginations for playing a game, you know, you've heard the drill from people that make this argument.

Didn't have to go to college, well, they had to go, but didn't have to attend class, had private tutors. As star athletes, the red carpet's been rolled out for them. Who are they to complain. Especially when their protests insult the very people who are paying all the money that makes them wealthy. That would be the fans.

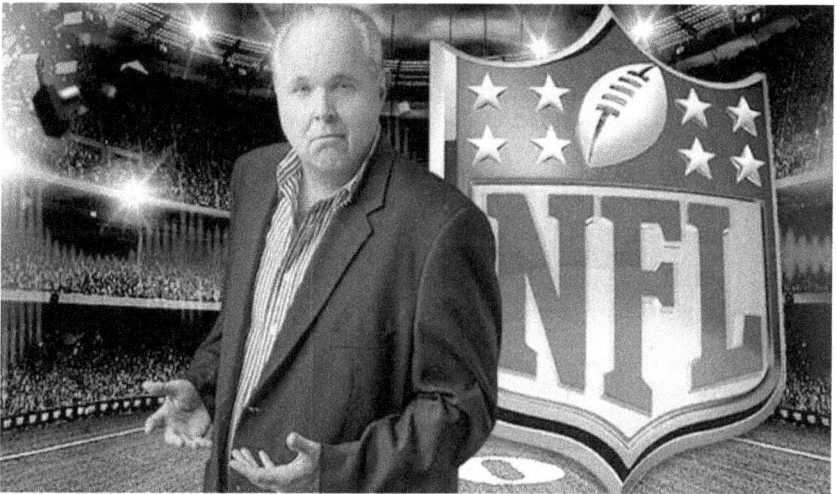

I don't know how successful it's going to be. But in reading a bunch of various NFL websites, I'm always fascinated to read the comments. Because you find left-wing insanity on full display there too. And, folks, I'm telling you, it is all around us. It has been building. It is being amplified. And it's being presented as normal. It's being presented, discussed, reported upon as quite normal, this madness and insanity.

So, I want to read an idea that a fan one of these websites had. As I read this, I want you to imagine yourself watching an NFL game on television or you are there, you are at an NFL stadium. Here is the fan's idea. What if, before the national anthem at every game, before the national anthem the stadium public address announcer observed a moment of silence for social injustice.

The PA announcer could read something like this: Ladies and gentlemen, the National Football League and the home team strongly believe in equality and social justice. As Americans and human beings, we should all strive to be kind to each other. And we should all treat each other with dignity and respect regardless of race, color, gender, creed, religion, or sexual orientation while in this stadium today and after we leave and go about our lives. We will now observe a moment of silence to reflect on those who have suffered injustice in our society. Thank you.

And then during that moment of silence for social injustice is when the players could kneel or raise a fist or lock arms. But when the anthem was played, all that had to end, and everybody had to stand with their hand over their heart and all that. Now, imagine yourself at a stadium where that is blared out over the PA system, especially as Americans and human beings, we should all strive to be kind to each other, and we should all treat each other with dignity and respect, what's gonna happen on the field in mere moments?

They're gonna try to kill each other, sheer brutality, organized brutality is gonna be occurring on that field mere seconds after the moment of silence for victims of social injustice. The fan here I'm sure is dead serious. And, by the way, the piece de resistance, he had a lot of fans agreeing with him thinking this is a great compromise.

Can you imagine yourself showing up at an NFL stadium and having to stand for a moment of silence before the anthem? Folks, this is more than just your average cultural evolution. This is more than just one generation being different than next or than its predecessor. The radicalization, the dumbing down — you know, what we hope is that every succeeding generation gets smarter, gets more productive, becomes wiser. That is not happening here.

We are witnessing before our eyes the dumbing down of our population. We see it in the absolute worthlessness of college degrees, not just the choices you can make in majors, but even if you take a traditional major, you don't know anything in it when you get your degree.

You've been taught a bunch of social justice garbage, you've been taught a bunch of multiculturalism, you have been taught a whole bunch of identity politics stuff, but you don't know, for example, if your degree is economics, you don't know it! You don't know anything about it. I find it worrisome because it's being done and it's happening here on purpose.

Closing the Chapter

For now, let's close this chapter by seeing the results of some polls that discuss how the American people have reacted to the Anthem fights.

According to the CBS poll, a little over half of respondents disapproved of players kneeling during the anthem, while 38 percent approved.

Similarly, in a HuffPost/YouGov poll, close to half of respondents felt the protest was inappropriate, while 36 percent thought it was appropriate.

In a separate CNN poll, when asked whether players kneeling during the anthem is the right or wrong thing, 43 percent of respondents said players were doing the right thing while 49 percent disagreed.

My advice would be that the players come up with another way of displaying outrage or they may ruin the goose that laid the golden egg. It may be that simple and wise.

One last piece of food for thought. A patriotic president, white or black, will most often choose country over everything else. I hope that overall this controversy helps us all be better Americans and be supportive of our country. For those players and for that matter all people that may not like America, there are a lot of countries that would love to have a few millionaires live there.

White or Black players who show disrespect for their country will be rewarded by regular people who have a love of country by voting with their green tickets (dollars), leaving the NFL and finding someplace else to spend their money—like helping University's build larger football stadiums. The NFL has no intrinsic right to exist.

I think the President, who is not a white racist would be fine with a natural solution to this current sports dilemma. The Rush Limbaugh designated solution seems pretty good to me. Remember once the goose realizes it no longer has to make those golden eggs, the choices for players, White and Black, are gone.

Chapter 7 Not Your Father's Democratic Party.

THE DEMOCRAT PARTY IS NO LONGER THE PARTY OF YOUR FATHERS

By Adding Anti-Free Speech, the Democrat Party has Now Become the 100% 'Anti' Party

Liberals Are Now 100% Anti-American

100% Anti-Freedom	100% Anti-Life
100% Anti-Catholic	100% Anti-Jew
100% Anti-Family	100% Anti-Truth
100% Anti-Business	100% Anti-Growth
100% Anti-Free Enterprise	100% Anti-Gun
100% Anti-Constitution	100% Anti-Patriotic
100% Anti-Responsibility	100% Anti-Liberty
100% Anti-Legal Immigration	100% Anti-God
100% Anti-Character	100% Anti-Energy

More and more pundits admit that this is not your father's Democratic Party. I am still a Democrat though a reluctant one for sure. I can't stand all the hate and the lying and the lack of concern for all Americans, especially white Americans. The Democratic Party now represents all fringe factors including illegal aliens as nothing is more important to Democrats than holding power and having their boot on the neck of every day American citizens who have yet to leave the Party.

There are many wimpy white males in the Democrat Party, even though the Democrats are conducting a war on Whites. Why are they doing this you may ask. The answer is as simple as the fact that there are more white male Republicans than white male Democrats, but it is even more than that. It has to do with power. White males are more likely citizens who understand America, want to work in high paying jobs, and who resist when Democrats using groupthink channels tell them what they can and cannot do.

Additionally, since very few white males ever came to America from south of the border, and since birds of a feather flock together, white males in America are not so easy to bowl over as all other races and/or nationalities. How else can one explain that in most elections the Dems are guaranteed over 90% of the black vote. It has almost always been this way but much moreso today than yesterday.

For example, no Democratic presidential nominee has ever received less than 82 percent of the black vote since Kennedy's 68 percent in 1960. And in the past 80 years, no Republican presidential nominee has done better than Eisenhower's 39 percent in his 1956 reelection bid. Of course, Blacks are beginning to rebel these days as they look and see that their lot has not improved much with all of that Democratic allegiance. And now with Trump doubling his approval from Blacks to 30%, there are pundits who are suggesting that the days of a guaranteed Black vote are over for Democrats.

The radical Democratic agenda and its major flirtation with socialism is not helping Blacks one bit but the fact that the Black unemployment rate is at a historical low in this Trump era, is helping Blacks take notice that Trump is not a racist. Even though Blacks know this for themselves, the ever-biased drive-by media are finding one non-issue after another to label Trump and all white males as racist.

Things are changing in America and some of the changes are for the good and some are for the bad. One of the major changes has been caused by major increases in immigration – legal and illegal. Neither Blacks nor Whites are happy with the Democrat position on immigration. An increasing number of Americans on the left do not believe in any limits: Some of us believe that within prescribed limits, we should allow all those escaping poverty or violence into the United States, but we must maintain our country's integrity with strict border enforcement and of course a wall to add muscle to the enforcement.

Hillary Clinton when she led the Democratic Party was caught on tape saying that she does not believe in borders at all. She still does not. She speaks for the American left: In the past year, anti-white male leftists have marched in American streets demanding the abolition of ICE, the Immigration and Customs Enforcement agency. They say all Whites are racist, but that drumbeat falls on deaf ears with most Whites, especially Republican white males.

What would the left have us do about immigration?" Their posture makes their answer irrelevant. Their answer is "Nothing. All migrants are welcome any time. No borders, no wall, no enforcement, No ICE. Here are two new Democrat slogans:

1. "No Border, No Wall, No USA at all.
2. "America was never that great."

Sounds like what one would see in a going out of business sale. Are the Democrats going out of business soon?

What if?

Though the drive-by media will never report it, there are many of us, Black, White, Yellow, and Red, Liberals, Conservatives and Independents who do believe in borders. The reason we feel that way has nothing -- absolutely nothing -- to do with race or ethnicity. In other words, Whitey gets a pass on this. Nonetheless, we worry. The reason we worry so much about vast numbers of immigrants is that too many immigrants in too short a period of time will change American culture and values. Our concern is not rooted in xenophobia. However, pundits do suggest that it is rooted in *values-phobia*.

Today's immigrants, legal and illegal want their old country to set up shop just like everything about their old country existed in America. It can't happen. That's why this is an issue now? The vast majority of past immigrants changed *their* values, not America's values, when they came to this country. They came here to become American, not only in terms of language, citizenship and national identity but also in terms of values.

The brush may not be so broad as there are some, though not the majority of new immigrants who still do come here for the freedom and for the values. Most are looking for something from the citizens of America besides just a nice place to live and raise a family. They want to become American citizens to make their lives better without changing their values or country identity. The majority of today's immigrants from Latin America, for example, wish to become wealthier Latin Americans in America; not wealthy Americans.

It has been going on for too long. Millions if not tens of millions of people have been coming to America with non-American values -- essentially, values that permit them to be takers and not givers. They like big government and a welfare state. And thanks to the Democratic Party and the left, they don't skuttle these non-American values. The Democrats want them to know the benefits come from big government Democrats. The Republicans simply want to employ them for slave wages even if it means Americans are denied work opportunities.

We have noted that Democrats want no limit on immigration. Bring 'em all down. How many do your suppose of the 7,642,225, 657 that were alive in the world on August 11, 2018 between 4:30 and 5:00 EST might want to come to live in America Suppose just half of the world's population desired to settle in America and we have deployed the Democrats Open Borders plan. That would mean that only 3.8 trillion people would need to be added to the US population, which today is 325 million. With all the zeroes showing, that difference would be

3,800,000,000,000
3,025,000

Looks like that would mean a million times increase in the US population. Impossible!

Economist Nathan Smith wants open borders and he says no sweat to the US. The US will "endure and flourish" if it chose to lay out 2,000 miles of welcome mats rather than building a Trumpian wall. Smith predicted the U.S. could handle an influx of 150-200 million immigrants over a span of several decades. Where do the 3.8 trillion go when they find out they can get to the US without ever having to be a citizen?

There are many conservatives that think it has already gone too far with legal and illegal immigrations causing the US welfare needs to swell. What is wrong with the United States being the nice sized country that it is?

Meanwhile the Trump White House is playing games to get the wall and most conservatives want none of what they are selling. The wimpy Republicans can do what they want but won't. Instead they take it on the chin from the Democrats and smile. The recent proposal expands the amnesty from the 700,000 beneficiaries of DACA to a larger pool of 2 million, in exchange for more resources and legal authorities at the border and changes in the legal-immigration system.

Conservatives are not looking at a Trump broken-promise with eagerness and are thus not enthusiastic about the larger amnesty, which is a significant political concession. It will present a real administrative challenge to U.S. Citizenship and Immigration Services. The White House is willing to go all the way and give the so-called Dreamers a pathway to citizenship. Conservatives are 100% against this move.

The problem is trust. Any amnesty, especially one this large, is a break from what has been a fundamental principle of immigration conservatives, Blacks and Whites: Establish a functioning system of enforcement before any amnesty potentially draws more illegal immigrants here by sending the message that they might be able to stay. The gains in enforcement and a tighter legal system would have to be substantial to make this departure worthwhile.

The White House wants its $25 billion for border enforcement, and new resources for immigration agencies, and changes in law. For example, the White House wants to eliminate the visa lottery and end family categories except for spouses and minor children.

These represent large-scale reforms to the system that would, if immediately implemented, quickly reduce the number of green cards issued by a third or more. The possibility of our do-nothing 2018 Democrat-bossed Congress signing up for such a rapid change is small and Republicans are ready to do nothing rather than pick a fight with the Democrats.

My suggestion is that we bring the measure to fund the wall to the floor and vote on it right away. Republicans who vote no and of course Democrats who vote no should be known to the voters. Let them pay at the ballot box. Let's get rid of them in 2018 or 2020 at the latest rather than keep them around to mess things up over the next several years.

The solution for 60 million illegal interlopers in the US is easy to achieve but we need a Congress first that wants to solve the problem. In Chapter 8, I introduce two solutions that together actually solve the problem with 60 million illegal interlopers residing in the US and in so doing it solves both DACA and Sanctuary Cities at the same time. Americans will love it; but politicians unfortunately seem to like having the issue rather than a fair solution for the country. .

Chapter 8 Solving the Problem of 60 Million Illegal Interlopers

Illegal immigration numbers are huge

In February 2004, Arizona Senator John McCain recognized via Border Patrol reports that nearly four million people crossed our borders "illegally" each year following the Reagan amnesty in 1986. Nonetheless, the fraudulent press insists that the total count of illegal immigrants residing in the United States is eleven million, a mathematical impossibility if Border Patrol figures are to be believed. And of these millions of foreigners, countless amounts receive welfare while, contrary to popular mythology, very few actually work in agriculture.

John McCain was not the only person in Congress who has known the real numbers of illegal immigrants in the country. Today, in addition to illegal border crossings, the largest source of illegal aliens is visa overstayers. They come on a work or student visa or even a travel visa. They like America. They stay. We let them. Democrats fight ICE to let them alone. They live in the shadows. Meanwhile people in their own country who have been to the US Embassy are waiting in line for years. We have an unfair system and overall each illegal person that we get in our country has committed a crime.

There may be as many as 60 million and perhaps more illegal foreign nationals living in the United States today. While some individuals in this group may contribute to our society, on balance this is outweighed by the group's overall negative effect on our resources, whether they be drained by government assistance, lost employment opportunities for American citizens, or criminal offenses. It is amazing how effective the fake-ID business is in turning illegal aliens into fake citizens who are thus enabled to enjoy American rights and privileges.

The best solution by far is to help them relocate back to their home country. Instead of spending $500 billion per year on welfare and other services, if we invested the money in their home towns, the dividends for interlopers and American citizens would be huge. mil

According to the 2011 GAO report entitled "Criminal Alien Statistics," the cost of crimes by illegal foreign nationals is $8.1 billion per year, and that's without even considering the incomprehensibly larger emotional toll this takes on families whose priceless loved ones can never be replaced. Regular Americans never asked for this. This problem came from corrupt politicians trying to get more voters for the Democratic Party or to do favors for big Republican donors to satisfy their perceived need for cheap labor.

If I were elected Senator or Congressman, I would introduce two pieces of legislation that will solve this problem of illegal residents in the shadows once and for all. Besides many other benefits, it stands to save the U.S. over $1 Trillion per year in addition to major reductions in crime. The two solutions are known as pay-to-go and the resident visa program. The solutions are so simple and understandable, it is hard to conceive of the fact that they are logical and workable and will in fact solve the problem in the best way.

Immigration law says we deport everybody who enters illegally or overstays their visas. That law is on the books. We need no other law but administration after administration before Trump has called off the dogs and in fact they have given illegal aliens more rights than American citizens. A paltry portion are sent back and that is why the number approaches 60 million interlopers residing in the shadows today. It is unhealthy for America and Americans.

Pay-to-Go

Nothing in life is free unless you come to America illegally. It costs taxpayers $30,000 per year on the average, per illegal alien in America. I have a way of keeping all the money back in the treasury each year and reuniting families at US expense in their home countries. Here's how Pay-to-Go, a program used successfully across the globe would work in America.

Each illegal resident and their dependent children, who signs up for Pay to Go, on the way back to the home country, would receive a one-time $20,000 stipend plus the individual expense back to the home country. With a cost of $30,000 per year to support unwelcome interlopers, the taxpayer savings begins year one and continues at $30,000 per year forever. Not a bad deal for Americans and a great deal for interlopers wanting a free ride back home.

The program therefore quietly accommodates family reunification in the home country. A family of five for example, could do quite well back home after receiving $100,000 in stipends from Uncle Sam. Reuniting families in their own countries is a good idea for them and for America. The savings in welfare means there is no cost in year one and in year 2, the savings equal $30,000 for each person who "goes." back home, never to return. That's it and when they are gone they are gone. No more shadows. No more crime from them.

Resident Visa

Not everybody willingly will leave the US for any amount. Bleeding heart Democrat liberals who for years advocated open borders would not want to send people home for any reason other than they requested to go home. They want the votes but can't say it, so they will say that it is unfair. Consequently, we needed to make Pay-to-Go voluntary and create a program for those not willing to take the offer.

Those who do not want to leave the US can sign up, be vetted, and eventually be approved for what we call a *Resident Visa*. The first-year cost for the visa for each interloper, man, woman, and child, will be $200.00. The #200 covers vetting and administrative costs in year one. It will be renewable every year thereafter for a $100.00 annual in which the visa holder's record will be updated with changes from the prior year. Visa recipients must apply in person each year as they are not and never will be citizens.

To get a Resident Visa, a former interloper would agree to all stipulations after registering. Stipulations would include full initial vetting; onsite renewal vetting; keep existing jobs; new jobs for Americans first; no voting; no citizenship; no welfare and no freebies of any kind. Everybody would not be automatically approved. After vetting, those not approved for the resident visa program may use the Pay-to-Go program to aid in their relocation.

The two programs would mean 100% of the illegal interloper population would be registered, vetted, approved or assigned to the Pay-to-Go program or deported with no benefits. With such participation from all illegal residents, in one year, there would be no more illegal residents that anybody was protecting as they could all be out of the shadows.

Estimates are as high as $500 billion per year cost savings in total for those who either choose to go or for those who choose to stay using the no-welfare resident visa. Another $500 billion will be reclaimed over time for lost wages. Additionally, if we can figure a way for countries to reclaim their criminals, there is another $8.1 billion to be recovered.

Once the program is in effect, there would be no more illegal aliens in the country. Resident Visa holders would be legal and so there would be no shadows. There would be no need for DACA and no need for Sanctuary cities Let me repeat that. All issues with DACA would be over and Sanctuary Cities would be a thing of the past because there would be no shadows and no illegal interlopers in America. They would either be gone or hold Resident Visas.

There are lots of other ways to expand the Resident Visa program to help America in handling its legal immigrants. These are explored in other Brian W. Kelly books

Amazon.com / author / brianwkelly

Chapter 9 Are Whites Being Left Behind in America?

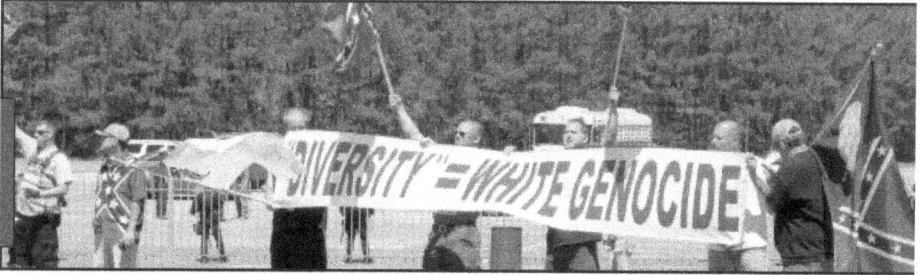

Whites are not happy about being called racists and White Supremist. Remember please that the KKK is not a white Republican group. White Supremist organizations, such as the KKK began with the Democratic Party. Senator Robert Byrd of West Virginial for example was a US Senator and a grand master in the Klan.

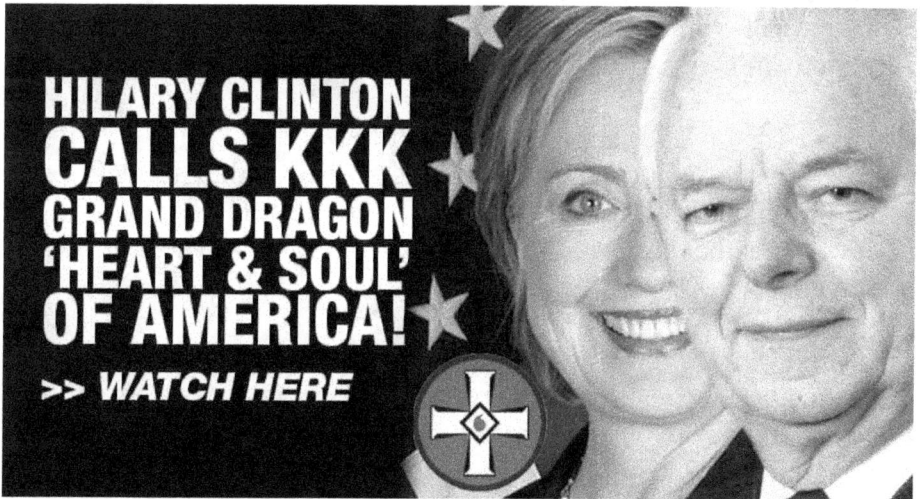

The pundits on the left believe that as America Changes, it makes Whites anxious and, in some ways,, Whites feel left behind. I think this is claptrap as the Whites I know do not buy the ideas that the labels of the corrupt press and the liberal progressives have any real meaning other than agitating minorities. The press tool that is most often used of course is fake news.

Whites are not pleased with what they see as Demographic shifts across the country and they are not pleased that goofy politicians such as Nancy Pelosi snidely suggest that Donald Trump et al want to Make America White Again. Right now, 62% of this country founded by Whites is white. So, why should the majority of the people in this country want to change America into a black, yellow, brown, or red country? You tell me. It makes no sense.

Nonetheless the fake new drumbeat of the press tells us that the demographic shifts rippling across the nation are fueling fears that white culture and standing are under threat. Is this a self-fulfilling prophecy?

For decades the Democrats have used race, religion & gender to divide the population and they are doing it again with their War on Whites.

Democrats suggest that Donald Trump's appeals to working-class White Americans have no doubt stoked racial tensions. How is that? By helping them make more money, Black and White alike, or by helping them get jobs?

They say Trump's popularity among White voters has also put an unexpected spotlight on their grievances—whether they feel left behind by globalization and immigration or resentful of an elite political class that seems to ignore them. OK if this is true, it is not a White issue?

Democrats ask if poor white Americans suddenly feel more disgruntled than ever, or are the rest of us just now paying attention? Let me answer that. Whites are disgruntled only by the Democrats always coming up with a divisive issue to feed their agenda and then the press swears to it.

Another question I'd ask is if there is a blow-up, how much has to do with economic factors versus matters of race or, simply, health? And what does it all mean for American politics—in 2016 and beyond? Every now and then somebody makes a mistake and tells the truth.

Susan Glasser, editor at left leaning Politico says "I'd love to just jump right in and ask "What is going on with America's White people, and how much is that driving the Trump phenomenon in this year's election? What I see in America today is anti-White bigotry by Black people. Black History Month is a racist gesture. If we have a Black History month, then we need a White History month and a Native American History month and an Asian History, etc." Well, the truth may hurt leftist causes, but the truth is the truth regardless of who it offends.

The fact is that for decades, examining race in America simply meant the researcher focused on the advancement and struggles of people of color. In this framework, being white was simply the default. After all today's 62% number for the white population is the lowest number ever. We got here from 1940 when the % of Whites was 90%.I agree that every other race or ethnic group was "other-ized," and matters of race were the problem and province of people of color.

In an era in which we had the first post-racial president and now a president who is accused every day by racist Democrats of being racist, the question of what it means to be white in America has increasingly been put under a microscope. Yet no matter what the scope says, the corrupt fake news press reports in a way that makes all Whites, especially white males look bad.

In this book, we have used the figure of 62% as the percentage of the population that is white. There was a time that white, yellow, and black were the only three races. That's how I grew up. This means that White Americans, including *White Hispanics* constitute the majority, with a total of about 246,660,710, or 77.35% of the population as of 2014. In 2014, non-Hispanic Whites totaled about 197,870,516, or 62.06% of the U.S. population.

If this analysis were of Mexico, and their numbers were the following: Hispanics and Latinos represent 90% of the population of Mexico as of 1940, whereas, in 2014, the number fell to 62%. What would their reaction be? Let's say that Whites were sneaking into Mexico at an alarming rate and that soon the White population was expected to overcome that of the Mexican segment?

Would Mexican authorities take action to save the culture of Mexico so that foreign cultures did not change life in the country by any measurable means. If Mexico took action under those circumstances or its Hispanic/Latino population took action on its, own, would the press declare their actions racist? Please read that paragraph again and ask if Whites in America are justified in having some angst?

Millennials often are tracked separately in surveys as the pundits do not see them as subscribing to traditional norms. So, perhaps the judgments of American millennials might be less biased than the general population. Perhaps!

Well, in a survey, half of white millennials say discrimination against Whites is as big a problem as discrimination against people of color. Of course, it is—but the fake news press fights discrimination against people of color whereas it fans the seeds of discontent regarding discrimination or just bad feelings against Whites

Most white millennials don't think minorities are taking their jobs, but nearly half believe that discrimination against Whites is a problem. In similar surveys, 27 percent of African-Americans and 27 percent of Latinos agreed, and a little over 20 percent of Asian-Americans agreed.

With all of the facts coming out, Whites have reason for concern and it is not just that they have become a favorite target of the leftist press. For the first time in US history, white Americans are faced with the prospect of becoming a minority in their "own country." Think about that. It does cause angst if one dwells on it.

There are many in our diverse, multicultural cities who may well celebrate the "browning of America." In their own racist closet, they see this as a welcome step away from "white supremacy." There is no way anybody can talk about this without admitting that large numbers of American Whites, as the percentage slides lower and lower, are more anxious about this phenomenon than ever before-- whether they admit it or not.

Strengthening the notion that demographic changes are substantial and significant, a 2012 study showed that more than half of white

Americans believe that "Whites have replaced Blacks as the 'primary victims of discrimination'."

Moreover, most Whites find the ever increasing "brown" population, spawned by illegal entry or overstay as the big problem for the shift.

In another survey, 43% of black Americans do not believe America will ever make the changes necessary to give Blacks equal rights. Showcasing the fact that people are blaming other races more and more, and the fact that the last president was 50% black but professed his blackness, and the current president is white-only, and he is more or less quiet on his own race but is picked on continually by the press as being a racist. This big divide has left us with a very troubling statistic in that hate crimes have increased 20% in the wake of the 2016 election.

When any group feels threatened, they often retreat into tribalism. When certain groups feel mistreated and disrespected, it is natural for them to close ranks and come together, becoming more defensive, more punitive, and inclined to be more us-versus-them.

In America today, every group feels this way to some extent. There are differences and the press tries to accentuate the differences and not the same-ness and that adds to the angst. Whites and Blacks, Latinos and Asians, men and women, Christians, Jews, and Muslims, straight people and gay people, liberals and conservatives – all feel their groups are being attacked, bullied, persecuted, discriminated against. Whites, once in their own safe haven, are now at the top of everybody's hit list, especially Democrats and the left-leaning corrupt press.

The more a group hears the complaints of another group, the more they feel threatened and voiceless. They are also often met by another group's derision because it discounts their own feelings of persecution – but such is the norm in political tribalism.

This–combined with what analysts suggest is record levels of inequality–is why we now see identity politics on both sides of the political spectrum. And it leaves the United States in a perilous new situation: almost no one is standing up for an America without identity politics, for an American identity that transcends and unites all the country's many subgroups.

To get this job done, we need an honest press that does not serve as a healer, and, does not take sides. If this corporate controlled press can't do it, American needs a new fledgling media to be taking the people's issues and causes seriously without bias.

It always helps to read the inspirational words of Dr. Martin Luther King when we are looking for some answers on race relations. Many of us can still recall in his most famous speech that King Jr proclaimed: "When the architects of our republic wrote the magnificent words of the Constitution and the Declaration of Independence, they were signing a promissory note to which every American was to fall heir. This note was a promise that all men – yes, black men as well as white men – would be guaranteed the unalienable rights of life, liberty, and the pursuit of happiness."

King's ideals captured the imagination and hearts of the public and led to real change. His words transcended group divides and called for an America in which skin color does not matter. We need the Fourth Estate more than ever to do its job well. And, we could use a reincarnation of a spirit such as that of Dr. Martin Luther King.

We have learned that once identity politics gains momentum, it inevitably subdivides, giving rise to ever-proliferating group identities demanding recognition. The more groups, the more differences and issues among the groups Today, there is an ever-expanding vocabulary of identity on the left. Facebook now lists more than fifty gender designations from which users can choose, from genderqueer to intersex to pangender. I do not understand how this helps anything.

I once thought that regular people would not tolerate all the leftist crap coming from the Democratic Party, but the leaders used team tactics to suck their lemming followers into loving the Party—often more than loving themselves. It is a fact that the Left is always trying to outleft the last Left. Very little progress has been made in "can't we all get along." It is like an "Oppression Olympics," which fragments all groups and sets them against each other. Very little new thought is bringing groups together today We may preach the value of inclusivity as still being the ultimate goal, however, the contemporary Left is pointedly exclusionary. That does not help.

During a *Black Lives Matter* protest at the DNC held in Philadelphia in July 2016, a protest leader announced that "this is a black and brown resistance march," asking white allies to "appropriately take [their] place in the back of this march." Think about that, please. . .

Cultural appropriation and identity politics

There is this relatively new idea that there is a war on "cultural appropriation," and that it is rooted in the belief that groups have exclusive rights to their own histories, symbols, and traditions. Thus, many on the left today would consider it an offensive act of privilege for, say, a straight white man to write a novel featuring a gay Latina as the main character. I won't focus on that, but we have to watch in life how we treat our friends.

Identity politics has delivered few rewards to the Left. There is a share of unhappiness about the direction this notion has taken. There are those for example who are very upset by the focus on cultural appropriation. In my research, I read about a progressive Mexican American law student who netted this out well, "If we allowed ourselves to be hurt by a costume, how could we manage the trauma of an eviction notice?" He added: "Liberals have cried wolf too many times. If everything is racist and sexist, nothing is. By the time Trump, a guy who the Left would call the real wolf, actually came along, he was unnoticed."

As we close in on concluding this chapter, we can deduce the most striking feature of today's right-wing political tribalism: the white identity politics that has mobilized around the idea of Whites as an endangered, discriminated-against group. No matter what words are used, Whites have taken notice and we are well aware that we all now have big targets on our backs. The Left has been relentless in their berating, shaming, and bullying and the more they agitate, the stronger the white males I know have become.

"The Democratic Party," said Bill Maher, "made the white working man feel like your problems aren't real because you're 'mansplaining' and check your privilege. You know, if your life sucks, your problems are real. When Blacks blame today's Whites for slavery or ask for reparations, many white Americans feel as though they are being attacked for the sins of other generations."

Some will tell you that today's white "problem" is simple but fundamental. While black Americans, Asian Americans, Hispanic Americans, Jewish Americans, and many others are allowed – indeed, encouraged – to feel solidarity and take pride in their racial or ethnic identity, white Americans have for the last several decades been told they must never, ever do so. It is taboo for White's to get together to commiserate or even plan a response. However, in the last few years, Whites are beginning to speak up and stick together. Hopefully, it will mean a resolution rather than a revolution with an escalation of the conflict. Nobody is really looking for a war.

Just like Blacks, Reds, and Yellows, White People want to see their own tribe as exceptional, as something of which to be deeply proud; that's what the tribal instinct is all about. For decades now, non-Whites in the United States have been encouraged to indulge their tribal instincts in just this way, but, at least publicly, American Whites have not. This is changing, and it is for the good—at least for Whites.

No more listening to those who tell the White community to suck it up--that their white identity is something no one should take pride in. "I get it," says Christian Lander, creator of the popular satirical blog Stuff White People Like, "as a straight white male, I'm the worst thing on Earth."

Amy Chua wrote in 2018 that just after the 2016 election, a former Never Trumper explained his change of heart in the Atlantic: "My college-age daughter constantly hears talk of white privilege and racial identity, of separate dorms for separate races (somewhere in heaven Martin Luther King Jr is hanging his head and crying) … I hate identity politics, [but] when everything is about identity politics, is the left really surprised that on Tuesday Election Day 2016), millions of white Americans ... voted as 'white'? If you want identity politics, identity politics is what you will get."

From <u>Political Tribes</u> by Amy Chua. Published by arrangement with Penguin Press, a member of Penguin Random House, LLC. Copyright © 2018 by Amy

Chapter 10 Hating Whitey

Hating Whitey and Other Progressive Causes Kindle Edition

by David Horowitz (Author

David Horowitz calls it as he sees it. You can get an awful lot of the essence of his book, *Hating Whitey and Other Progressive Causes* Kindle Edition by reading the free Description on the Web.

The anti-white racism of the Left remains one of the few taboo subjects in America. A former confidante of the Black Panthers and author of Radical Son, in his book, David Horowitz lays bare the liberal attack on "whiteness"—the latest battle in the war against American democracy. His passionate and candid account of contemporary racism reveals that the Cold War has come home, and it is a race battle.

Ideological hatred of Whites is now a growth industry, boosted by "civil rights" activists and liberal academics. These once-youthful radicals, now white haired, and entrenched in positions of power and influence, peddle a warmed-over version of the Marxist creed that supported the communist empire and excuses intolerance to the point of thuggery. Betraying the legacy of Martin Luther King, this alliance of black civil rights leaders and white radicals threatens to undermine America's moral, political, and economic institutions.

Words from a famous White Guy: *"You better watch out!"*

Mr. Horowitz acknowledges that America's unique political culture is the creation of white European males, primarily English and Christian. In other words, it was not trade ships from Africa that discovered the New World. These very men and their heirs have led the world in abolishing slavery and establishing the principles of ethnic and racial inclusion.

Undeterred, so it seems, by America's Anglo-Saxon pedigree, people of every race and creed still flock by the millions to these shores for a share of our unparalleled rights and opportunities. Yet, with staggering hypocrisy, a clique of racial warlords and academic coffee-breath malcontents indicts our every institution for racial oppression.

No stranger to ideological combat, Mr. Horowitz anticipates the standard charges of racism and sexism—wearisome bromides reflexively hurled at dissenters from the party line. Undaunted, in his book, he boldly grapples with contemporary racism in all its forms.

This book is easily downloadable and readable with the Cloud Reader. Just type the title and access kindle and for $2.99, it's yours. I did it. You can too.

Horowitz is a contributor to Web daily Salon.com and he is also editor of Frontpagemag.com. He is a former 1960's radical who once helped run a Black Panther elementary school. He describes his past idealism based in the idea of "equality for all," and a current conservatism grounded in the same idea.

Of course, this book is about the '90s, and "equality" for Horowitz now means the complete end of Affirmative Action, and the end of a "Leftist McCarthyism" that silences conservative voices on college campuses.

Horowitz is right on the Left's perspective on "Whitey." Mainstream liberal leaders like Jesse Jackson and Cornel West have publicly appeared with Nation of Islam leaders at events like the Million Man March (remember that), thereby tacitly condoning the anti-Semitic and anti-white rhetoric that they spew. Ergo, Horowitz argues, racism against Whites by Blacks is often ignored and winked at in this country. But it is definitely there, and it definitely can be classified as racism.

One must ask why does the predominantly liberal media ignore and dismiss this non-White on White racism with such vigor. Because they can! Horowitz quickly makes his point cut and dry on what we might call reverse racism and he does it so easily one would think the real daily news would be full of reported incidents. But the fake news outlets remain mum as if they like the chicanery they create by not telling the whole truth.

Look at OJ, Horowitz says. Look at the "black rage" defense that juries have actually swallowed in some murder cases. Look at the historical revision that has lionized the Black Panther Party, a group that Horowitz continually describes as a group of murderous street thugs. Horowitz makes some great points in his book, but he does not tell us enough about why this form of racism is somehow more often ignored or even forgiven than reported by the MSM, in ways to point out its ugliness.

There are many immigrant groups that sailed to America in the last 500 years, only one group came in shackles. Horowitz often compares the poor circumstances of the Blacks to that of Asian immigrants, Jewish citizens, and other groups. In all fairness, however, this was not a period piece and did not highlight the Civil War and Reconstruction.

He does not choose to highlight that African-Americans are racially marked in ways other oppressed groups are not, and he did not spend a lot of words, and in some ways seems to deny the relevance of slavery and that over 150 years after the Civil War, its root cause continues to affect the USA.

For his own reasons, Horowitz does not see the existence of "institutional racism," which is, simply, racism within the laws and protocols of the state and its public institutions. I of course see it clearly. He actually makes a convincing case that being Black would not hurt anybody's chances of getting into Harvard if Affirmative Action were completely eliminated. I'm not too sure about that!

This conveniently narrow take on such a complex issue is reflected clearly in David's near-unconditional worship of our Founding Fathers. I have a similar notion about the founders and have expressed it in a number of Patriotic books about the founding and the founding documents. He does cite the issues of America and England and their major differences.

He writes about these two countries being "…the nations that led the world in abolishing slavery and establishing the principles of ethnic and racial inclusion." Critics of Horowitz suggest he did not take enough issue with the slavery issue during the founding. I think he did well and I think that without the group of founders that sacrificed everything including family for our country, I am not about to damn them. I thank them. The worst thing I can imagine is being a British Citizen.

As noted previously in this book, there are people, such as the founders who became so immersed in the benefits of slavery that though inside they knew it was wrong, everybody was doing it. That is not an excuse, but it explains how good white men might actually without malice operate in ways that others see as evil. 1

Horowitz clearly understands that racism is not a thing of the past. allows for "individual" racists, of course, but suggests that this type of racism does not much affect the way people are allowed to live their lives.

Horowitz defends Ward Connerly, for example, one of a few conservative black spokesmen for California's Civil Rights Initiative and his writing in this regard is quite admirable. He accurately paints the vocal college students who shout Connerly down and intimidate him wherever he appears, as hypocrites who seem to conveniently forget the principles of the First Amendment. Additionally, because he is not a liberal, they conveniently forget about Connerly's *blackness*.

Liberals would find such scenes embarrassing if they were not sold on Pelosi and Schumer. If Affirmative Action is truly justifiable, then why all the smokescreens? The silencing? The shouts of "Uncle Tom"? Where are the facts and logical arguments? It's completely patronizing and borderline racist to assume that if an African American holds conservative views, then he or she must be a puppet of white conservatives. Yet, let me say again that the Left and the Press and the Democrats have little use for the truth.

A full reading of the Horowitz book is necessary to grab its fullness. Halfway through *Hating Whitey*, the author seems to abandon the issue of race. What he chooses to explain is the ways in which the New Left is inextricably attached to Soviet-style Communism. Russia! Russia! Russia!. No Ipana!

He draws up a veritable Red List of sympathizers. Some on the far left would suggest that his big fault here is making almost no distinction between socialists and Stalinists. They would suggest that in this, he has fired off a dangerous series of cheap shots. Not so! The Left is so far off the true path that sometimes shock treatment of issues is needed to get the hoi polloi, aka the regular people in society to be awakened to how things really are.

Horowitz has great vision in that he often equates the questioning of American policies and values with dangerous anti-Americanism. It is not that one cannot question a government gone bad. In fact,

Americans are encouraged by the founders to use their Second Amendment privileges to forcibly take down a government that is no longer *for the people*.

Horowitz spent time with the Black Panthers and this group is still operational. He has a recurring invective in this book against the Black Panther Party and only he would have his great insights. Of course, this group was anti-American, and he cites the many "armchair Communists" (as Horowitz calls certain liberal scholars—I call them coffee-breath professors). They sit and judge everything with a progressive / leftist rule book and they convince the minds of mush students that the Marxist philosophies are the best. No wonder our kids lose perspective for twenty years after having to deal with the coffee-breath professors in the anti-American academia.

Writing critics, especially those on the Left might characterize Horowitz' work as a loosely woven string of essays, but what do they know. I've written 172 books so far. 99% are fact-based non-fiction. Sometimes strings of essays are a good style as not everybody needs a full dose of everything. Would they even consider defending "Whitey" as the Whites in America today are being attacked? It does not seem like the press or the Democratic Party will ever come to the defense of Whitey, as more than likely, he is a dirty Republican.

Horowitz' rightfully links Leftism with un-Americanism. He makes his point about Stalinist bogeymen so many times that it is tough to miss.

Bill Clinton, the first suck-up for a black vote president, aka The First Black President is a clear Horowitz demon. *Clinton and the Chinese* is the choice that the author uses to point out how American nuclear safety was threatened as we know from the few honest news reports of those times.

My hat is off to Mr. Horowitz for a job well done.

Each chapter in this book helps us through the theme of the spoof book title, *White People Are Bad! Bad! Bad!* It is safe to say that no reasonable conservative would contend that racial discrimination does not exist anymore today, so to some extent it seems we must concede white privilege is a real phenomenon, though we may disagree over both the degree of its impact and how it is applied. One thing is for sure. It is a bad game played by Democrats who will do anything to retaliate for their 2016 presidential loss, and a corrupt press. No thanks, Omaha! Thanks A lot!

1

Chapter 11 Trump's Angry White Men

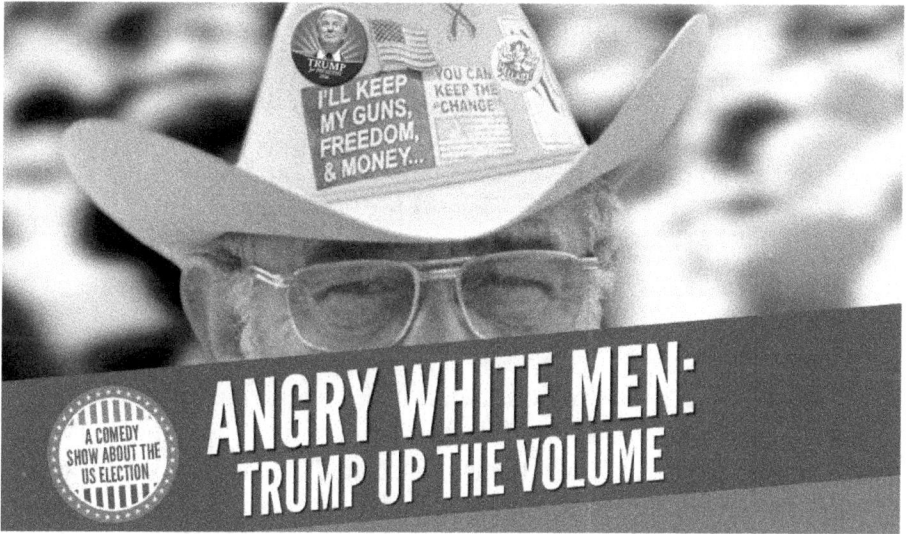

Why there is more anger than you think

Other than being called a *white male racist*, a *white supremist*, or any of the other slang negatives used by leftists and liberal progressives to describe an American White man today, statistics pre-Trump for years pointed to conspiracy theories, mediocre wages and a deeply held belief that white males are anything but racist. We, the Whiteys of the US, are not racist as a group. In fact, we do not even operate as a group and are not part of groupthink. American white males are individuals. Amen!

This article about Trump is over 2 years old but the ideals have not changed.

https://www.theguardian.com/us-news/2016/jan/08/angry-white-men-love-donald-trump

This is a perspective about the angry white men (with due cause) who flocked to Donald Trump as a potential president bold enough to address and help cure America's eight-year-long sickness in which regular white people had to suck it up because they had no say and no input.

The essence of this chapter comes from a Donald Trump speech at a campaign rally in Nashua, New Hampshire. There were photograph by Brian Snyder/Reuters. This is so short, to capture the great writing of the author, I will include it all. Here it is. Enjoy!

> Michael has presumably had a rough day. Nine hours working as an exterminator takes a physical toll on the 45-year-old, who didn't go to college, makes $33,000 a year, and relies on a steady swarm of pests to pester people in his 90% rural county.
> But home, with a glass of wine and Fox News, he's excited to hear from the only candidate who's making any sense these days: Donald Trump.
>
> Michael is technically fictional, but he's created entirely from fact. The story of Trump's success is, in some ways, the story of the many American Michaels. Frustrated white men who reject the stories offered to them and admire leaders who feel the same.
>
> White Americans feel more angry than black Americans, according to a November survey of 3,257 US adults by Esquire and NBC. White people were more likely than black people to say their current financial situation isn't what they thought it would be when they were younger, and they were also more likely to put that down to difficult circumstances rather than "wrong choices."
>
> When asked whether they ever hear or read anything on the news that makes them angry, white respondents were more likely than black ones to say they felt angry at least twice a day. There were gender differences too – men were more likely than women to say that they felt angry about the treatment of white men.
>
> Trump understands these white men – or at the very least, he understands that these white men want a politician who understands them. It was these voters that Trump was speaking to when he said last year:
>
> "And if you look at black and African American youth, to a point where they've never done more poorly. There's no spirit."

This is more than just opportunism – Trump gets it. Of course, the history of American politicians is the history of many, many white men, but there's something unique about Trump's whiteness and his masculinity. He is distinctly unashamed of either trait, and is unwilling to even pay lip service to the notion that they were beneficial to his success. In a 1989 NBC interview, for example, he made his point:

A well-educated black has a tremendous advantage over a well-educated white in terms of the job market. I think sometimes a black may think they don't have an advantage or this and that … I've said on one occasion, even about myself, if I were starting off today, I would love to be a well-educated black, because I believe they do have an actual advantage.

[Think about it folks, are they the words of a *racist?*]

Liberals may respond with rolled eyes or outrage, but for men like the hypothetical Michael, quotes like these are evidence that Trump is simply willing to state facts others are too cowardly to say. Michael still probably wouldn't think of himself as racist – 10% of white Americans think white Americans are racist. But 38% of those white Americans think black people are racist.

More than 20 years later, a Michael would probably still agree with the statement. When asked why Black Americans have worse jobs, incomes and housing on average than Whites, 45% of white Americans in 2012 said it was because "Blacks don't have the motivation or willpower to pull themselves out of poverty." If that is wrong, let's talk about it.

The fact that most media organizations do not repeat these beliefs – aka "facts" to some who hold them – merely entrenches the feeling that the mainstream, "lamestream" media cannot be trusted.

The white man pathology inside the fandom of Sanders and Trump.

Though angry white men never expect that the media will ever support their cause, there are always glimmers and rays of hope. But after time passes, they go nowhere. A 2014 study from Pew Research Center shows just how divided Americans are about the media.

Liberal progressives express trust in more media organizations than conservatives do and receive more sources and perspectives as a consequence. Of 36 organizations listed, Fox News stands out as the crucial source to 88% of conservatives who say that they trust the information they receive from the channel.

Social media is important too; the study shows that if Michael does exist, he would probably also be checking Facebook – where he would hear from close friends who are more likely to share his views.

This isn't just healthy skepticism– at times it's an entirely different version of the world. Whether you want to call them conspiracy theories or government secrets, a 2013 survey from Public Policy Polling shows these views tend to differ by political party too (though not all – 28% of Democrats and 28% of Republicans believe aliens exist).

Republicans were more likely to believe in Bigfoot, government TV mind control and diseases invented for pharmaceutical companies to profit than Democrats were. White Americans were more likely to believe those claims than Black Americans, and in most cases, men were more likely than women to believe the conspiracies listed in the survey.

One theory is particularly important: 37% of Americans think global warming is a hoax. That number rises to 39% when you only look at male respondents, 41% for white respondents and 58% for Republicans. With that in mind, it's easier to understand who the audience is when Trump makes statements like these:

Donald J. Trump(@realDonaldTrump)

The concept of global warming was created by and for the
Chinese in order to make U.S. manufacturing non-competitive.
November 6, 2012

It's not only what he says but the way he says it: Trump's writing
style echoes online forums and sites like knowthelies.com.

Trump uses short sentences. No commas needed. And
sometimes ALL CAPS.

With all this in mind, Trump's rising political fortunes aren't
surprising at all. Polling shows he is more popular among
Americans that are white than those who aren't, and more
popular among Americans with penises than those without.
Often, these white men are also working or middle class and
middle-aged – just like Michael.

Those men represent a significant voting block in a country
which is still 62% white. When those men want to hear from
someone who is willing to stand up for them, Donald Trump is
only too willing to oblige. And, when what's "right" is about
unapologetically refuting facts, Trump can't go wrong.

Chapter 12 Most Politicians Are Still White Men

The study also found most candidates running for office are white men. (ALAN DIAZ/AP)

A new study released Tuesday by the Reflective Democracy Campaign on the demographics of elected officials in the United States found white men hold a majority of positions at all levels of government. Considering that at one time after the founding, white men, save white women, represented close to100% of the population of America. Yet white men did not stop what they perceived to be non-white others from entering and taking challenging measures to become citizens of this great United States of America.

Despite white men, comprising only 31 percent of the population, 97 percent of all Republican elected officials are white, and 76 percent are male. Of all Democratic elected officials, 79 percent are white, and 65 percent are male, according to the study. So, why do White Democrats vote against other whites? I do not think I can explain that in this one book.

A factor in the discrepancy, RDC says, is a problem with who runs for office. Of Republican candidates, 73 percent are white men and 23 percent are white women. Men of color make up 3 percent of candidates and women of color make up 1 percent, according to the study.

Of Democratic candidates, 55 percent are white men and 27 percent are white women. Eleven percent are men of color and 6 percent are women of color. White women make up 31 percent of the population; men and women of color make up 19 percent of the population each. I am still puzzled as to how Democrats can adopt a 100% anti-white-male notion with 55% of white males being candidates for the DNC. Maybe they lie and say they are brown?

"Politics is not the kind of open, competitive playing field we'd like to think of it as. It's more like trying to be inducted into a fraternity," Brenda Carter, director of the Reflective Democracy Campaign, told The Washington Post. "I think the No. 1 problem is the political parties and other gatekeepers who choose candidates. I always say the parties are like hiring committees, and they're doing a really bad job of presenting voters with a range of candidates who look like the American people."

The power of incumbency is another "startling factor in the race and gender imbalance," according to the study. Fifty-two percent of elected officials run unopposed, of these, 87 percent are white, and 58 percent are Republicans.

One of the biggest hurdles for women and people of color who want to run for office is money, said Quentin James, co-founder of the Collective PAC, which recruits and supports progressive black candidates. Quentin said it is hard for these groups to compete with the fundraising networks of white candidates, the Post reported. "It's not a talent gap, it's a financial gap," James said. "There's just a ton of systematic problems, with campaign finance, with institutions not recruiting candidates of color that [candidates] have to overcome."

The research was commissioned in 2014 by the Women Donors Network, which researches and provides funding to efforts working to increase diversity in politics, and looked at more than 42,000 elected officials nationwide from the President to the county level. It compiled data from the 2012 and 2014 November general elections and analyzed more than 51,000 candidates by race and gender.

Why white people think they're the real victims of racism

The verdict

There is evidence in the official police-recorded figures that black Americans are more likely to commit certain types of crime than people of other races.

While it would be naïve to suggest that there is no racism in the US criminal justice system, victim reports don't support the idea that this is because of mass discrimination.

Higher poverty rates among various urban black communities might explain the difference in crime rates, although the evidence is mixed. There are few simple answers and links between crime and race are likely to remain the subject of bitter argument.

When you see a story with a headline like "New research finds that prosecutors give white defendants better deals than black defendants," you may not be surprised. After all, it's just one of a myriad of ways in which researchers have identified ongoing racial discrimination, whether it's in housing or employment or the way people are treated by law enforcement. On the other hand, you might dismiss it as fake news, knowing that the real victims of racial discrimination today are white people.

If that sounds silly to you, I have some bad news: There are millions of people who think that's what the state of racism in America is. According to a new poll from NPR, the Robert Wood Johnson Foundation, and the Harvard T.H. Chan School of Public Health, 55 percent of white Americans believe that Whites suffer from racial discrimination in America today. The respondents were not kidding. The press does not even know Whites exist.

This isn't the first time we've seen a poll result like that. Earlier this year, a poll from the Public Religion Research Institute found 52 percent of working class Whites saying discrimination against Whites is as big a problem as discrimination against Blacks and other minorities (though the number was smaller among Whites with higher education levels). And last year, Gallup found 43 percent of Whites saying discrimination against Whites is "widespread" in America.

What form is this discrimination against Whites supposed to take? Are they getting pulled over and searched by the police? Followed around by security guards in stores? Subjected to invidious stereotypes as people and institutions regard them not as individuals but primarily as undifferentiated members of a racial category? No, probably not. If you asked, a lot of those respondents would probably say "Affirmative action!", though in reality that affects only a tiny number of people. But, knowing it exists has negative consequences by itself.

So, affirmative action does play an important role in the feelings of many Whites, as both a symbol of how minorities supposedly get unearned benefits and as a vehicle by which old racial animus was modernized to become contemporary racial resentment, a socially unacceptable feeling replaced with one possible to air in polite company.

Let's take a trip down memory lane all the way back to 1990, when Republican Sen. Jesse Helms of North Carolina aired the infamous "white hands" ad in his bid for re-election against Harvey Gantt, an African-American who had been mayor of Charlotte:

Though Helms was a virulent racist, this ad is all about fair treatment for Whites: "You needed that job. You were the best qualified. But they had to give it to a minority because of a racial quota. Is that really fair?" The point was to give white voters a more practical explanation for their feelings, a language to talk about it that didn't sound nakedly racist.

My point in bringing up that vivid illustration is that for decades, conservatives have been relentlessly delivering a message to white voters that they are the true victims of discrimination. As a pair of researchers wrote last year:

> *Our research also suggests that among Whites, there's a lingering view that the American Dream is a "fixed pie," such that the advancement of one group of citizens must come at the expense of all the other groups. Whites told us they see things as a zero-sum game: Any improvements for black Americans, they believe, are likely to come at a direct cost to Whites. Black respondents in our surveys, meanwhile, report believing that outcomes for Blacks can improve without affecting outcomes for white Americans. [The Washington Post]*

The idea of any advancement for minorities coming at the expense of Whites gets constantly reinforced, nowhere more than on Fox News, the most important conservative media outlet, where white identity politics is always on the schedule. Yes, that is true, and I said it but Whites know that Fox is the only network of ten or so that treats conservatives fairly and mostly treats Whites fairly. Yet. Fox always tries to bring on the other (leftist) perspective. Conservatives do not report that they see a lot of "the other side" in leftist media outlets.

At Fox, for years, its foremost purveyor was Bill O'Reilly, who recently left the channel after it was revealed that he had settled lawsuits with a series of women claiming he had sexually harassed them. In his many years as the highest rated host on cable news, O'Reilly not only assembled a long record of racist statements, but told his viewers over and over again that Whites and Christians were victimized by a left that wielded awesome power to discriminate against them. Or as he put it once, "If you're a Christian or a white man in the U.S.A., it's open season on you."

Some of us who are not especially fans of O'Reilly would say that he was 100% right. Now that he is no longer a voice of reason out there, things have gotten worse.

Bill O had plenty of company in other conservative media, particularly in the Obama years. Leftists would say that hosts such as Rush Limbaugh would tell their listeners, "Obama's entire economic program is reparations" — in other words, stealing from virtuous Whites to bestow benefits on undeserving Blacks. The campaign against white America would be unrelenting, from the most powerful person in the country. " AS a White American, I can say that from my point of view I saw Obama as rejecting his white side and this seeded my distrust that he cared an iota for Whitey.

Back when, Glenn Beck was on Fix. " This president, I think, has exposed himself as a guy, over and over and over again, who has a deep-seated hatred for white people," said Glenn Beck. And he was coming for you. I studied Obama's work, and I believe that he was ready to come after me if his chosen successor had won. I did what I could to stop that from happening. I am proud to be white and Irish. But, if I were black, I suspect I would be proud to be Black and Ghanan.

Any other minority who ascended to a position of power was likely to be described by conservatives as a racist who would use that position to victimize innocent Whites. You might remember that when Obama nominated Sonia Sotomayor to the Supreme Court, conservatives charged not only that she was an unqualified affirmative action hire (of course), but that she was anti-white. "A white man racist nominee would be forced to withdraw. Latina woman racist should also withdraw," said Newt Gingrich.

After eight years of hearing those messages, it isn't surprising that many Whites felt that they were oppressed and held back, particularly if the circumstances of their own lives were not what they would have liked. Then along came Donald Trump.

What a breath of fresh air. In 2016, before the election, I wrote an essay about Donald Trump expressing my feeling about his being able to gain the nomination, and my hope for his victory.

I do not know why non-whites believed it was OK, whether somebody told them that they didn't even have to be shy about it anymore. It was now OK to be hard on the White Majority. Non-Whites were encouraged to proudly proclaim all those resentments — against racial minorities, against immigrants, against women — and rally behind the most unabashedly bigoted and vulgar candidate anyone had ever seen.

I like being white and have no reason to believe I should be something else. Some think that when Trump runs for re-election in 2 ½ years, we should not be surprised if his campaign is intensely racialized, as he realizes that getting all those white voters angry and riled up is his only path to victory. It'll sound awfully familiar. But like every position put forth by anti-white racist Democrats, it is designed to get voters to think something is wrong with Trump. There is nothing wrong with Trump, for sure, unless you believe that America was never great, and it cannot become great out of thin air because it was never great.

That America was never great, despite the founder's peril in facing England in the Revolution, is an outrageous slander about some of the greatest Americans this country has ever or will ever see again. I for one am so glad they came along to help us free our country from the yoke of the attachment cable to Mother England.

Chapter 13 No Borders; No Wall; No USA At All

If you were wondering if the new Democratic Party, the one that is anti-ICE, Open Borders, Pro Abortion, and many other things that you are not for, is just misinformed. Wonder no longer. In fact, add to the long list of negative attributes anti-American and downright nasty.

They matter only because it is the same Democrat Party in cahoots with the biased corrupt fake-news media who are telling all Americans to Hate Whitey, especially if Whitey is a male. Sooner or later, White Democrats still see that it is not only not your white father's party, the Democratic Party is not for you either.

Their protests may be nasty, and they may not make much sense, but despite that, they sure do not want to solve the hate problem in America. They love to foment hate, rather than solve its root cause. At the counter-protest on Sunday, August 12, 2017, there were no olive branches in the streets as nobody was asking for peace among brothers any time soon but there were a lot of white haters out there on the streets singing the newest hit song to warm up the Hate America contingent.

Antifa Chanted Death to America: 'No Borders! No Wall! No USA at All!' according to Breitbart. Open borders protesters and members of the left-wing anarchist group Antifa chanted death to America during a counter-protest in Washington, DC, on a Sunday in July 2018.

In a video by Breitbart News' Ian Mason, Antifa members and open borders activists can be heard and seen marching down streets throughout Washington, DC, demanding an end to the United States. That sounds like death to a lot of us. One must ask, "would it not be easier to just find a different country than to hunt down and kill all Americans?

Antifa — short for 'anti-fascist's, is the latest of named groups who hate all things American. They wear masks and riot gear and they are ready to smash the faces of anybody who does not think like them, especially Whitey. They are essentially a loosely affiliated, left-leaning highly racist v Whites, supposed anti-racist group that monitors and tracks the activities of supposed local neo-Nazis. But, they will go anywhere for a fight.

The Antifa anti-American movement has no unified structure or national leadership but it has emerged in the form of local bodies nationwide, particularly on the West Coast. But, they were out in full-force in Charlottesville on the 12th 2017 to supposedly counter a White Demonstration.

Some of the contingent groups, such as the 10-year-old Rose City Antifa in Portland, Oregon, the oldest antifa group in the U.S., are well-organized and active online and on Facebook, while its members are individually anonymous.

President Trump has singled out Antifa as part of what he calls the alt-left in his initial claim that "many sides" were to blame for violence in Charlottesville the weekend of Aug. 12, not just the neo-Nazis, KKK and white nationalists.

How is it pronounced?

"AN-tifa" with the emphasis on the first syllable, which sounds more like "on" in English than "an."

Here are some random ramblings from the march.

With 62% of Americans of White persuasion, one wonders what is there to gain for a group that is Democrat sponsored, radical, anti-White and anti-American? They won't win any elections any time soon. Some who watched the rally on Sunday 2018 suggested that it was very much what one would expect if the scene on the streets of Washington, D.C. was actually in Tehran.

Like radical Iranian Islamists, hundreds, if not thousands, of far leftists took to the streets of the nation's capital to chant for the end of America. President Trump's opinion was captured by the Trump Train:

The Trump Train  @The_Trump_Train

"Violent ANTIFA roaming the D.C. streets with wooden sticks chanting "No border, no wall, no USA at all"
6:02 PM - Aug 12, 2018

To repeat, "No border, no wall, no USA at all," was the main chant. They wore black and many for fear of recognition, concealed their faces. Americans on Sunday asked: "At what point is Antifa going to be deemed a domestic terrorist organization?

Pics of the March

Here is another post:

 SuperElite Johnny 50  @Johnny5024

#Antifa chants "No borders, no wall, no USA at all!" They want to destroy America. The Democrats must not be allowed to win in 2018. 7:10 PM - Aug 12, 2018

Members of the media were complaining the agitators were attempting to prevent them from covering their antics.

DeJuan Hoggard
✔ @DeJuanABC11

Protestors didn't want to be filmed and cut my photographer's audio cable cord. 12:26 PM - Aug 12, 2018 Charlottesville, VA

Twitter Ads info and privacy

ABC 11's DeJuan Hoggard reported one protests cut his photographer's audio cable cord.
An NBC crew was assaulted yesterday in Charlottesville.

Here are some random thoughts from Breitbart:

Gabriel G. Gator Liberty Rising Less Gov = More • 13 hours ago
The demon George Soros (anti-western civilization leftist Democrat) organizes, advertises, and funds these atrocities and the left runs amok on his dime. The U.S. left has become a roving pack of sociopathic monsters - this is why they lost in epic proportion in 2016. This is why they will continue to lose in future elections. I do, however, encourage the left to proceed forward using the same failed

incoherent logic; they do more damage to their nefarious cause by burning down a single small business than I could do with a million words.

Freedomring17 Gabriel G. Gator • 13 hours ago
This is a perfect clip for Republicans at midterms highlighting the left's Open Border Agenda, amongst other things like corporate capitalist censorship. Playing out nicely!

OCJoe Freedomring17 • 12 hours ago
I agree. Playing out very nicely. The Dems own all of this.

Danadee Freedomring17 • 11 hours ago
If the Republicans are smart enough to use it!!

John airconn danadee • 10 hours ago
Until they get rid of commie Ryan and China Mitch, they will not win as much as they could. !!

Bob Jones lane johnson 9 hours ago
We have never treated mortal enemies of the United States with the kid gloves we are using on Antifa and the Democrats. They should be dealt with as enemies that are dedicated to the overthrow of our nation. They are coming out and saying that publicly.

Siriusly Bob Jones • an hour ago
Since they like mobs, I think execution by an opposition mob would be fitting. Perhaps it will eventually come to that.

jpatriot18 Siriusly • 9 minutes ago
Perhaps?
We are on the precipice.
Only a matter if time.

Argentum lane johnson • 9 hours ago
Everyone wants to burn Iran for DEATH TO AMERICA chants
Burn Antifa first!

Michael James Allison Argentum • 4 hours ago
yep.

Bob Jones Billy Jack Soyboy Destroyer • 9 hours ago
With someone like Sleepy Sessions, don't count on any laws being
enforced. Trump could, and should, put a stop to the lawlessness we
see today.

Billy Jack Soyboy Destroyer Bob Jones • 8 hours ago
NO!

The government is not enforcing the law.
So the people need to reach down, squeeze their jewels till they swell
back up to normal, take the bull by the horns and do it themselves!
ENFORCE THE LAW!
Or cancel it completely so those of us with some stones can do what's
needed without fear of 20 trillion years in jail for hurting a
snowflake's feelings when they are trying to harm us.

Trying to overthrow the government used to be a serious crime.
Now, they chant about it in the streets and nobody does a damn
thing!

When do we say ENOUGH?!!!!??!!!!?!?!?!

Michiguy Madison Billy Jack Soyboy Destroyer • an hour ago
Chanting in the streets is protected free speech. Attacking people is a
crime. Lock up the ones who are violent.

I think we all get the point

Whites are pushing back quietly as this is still a White America.

Fox News Reports on the "Rally / Protest"

Though many Whiteys see Fox News as a money-making
organization whose new owners (the Murdoch Kids) would be happy
ideologically if somebody bought them out, they stay in ameliorating
the conservatives, so they can make more money. Knowing their real
hearts, many of us are waiting for Fox to say one day that they made
enough money on us, and now they are not going to give
conservatism another word. I hope not but who knows.

Regarding the rally v white supremacists, it was all over the news
yesterday, and Fox News was thankfully telling the truth. Hundreds
of counter-protesters, including Antifa, confronted a group of white-
nationalist demonstrators Sunday at the so-called "Unite the Right II"
march toward the White House -- and many pushed back as officers
tried to clear the area in the evening, triggering scuffles.

A passing thunderstorm forced the far-right demonstrators to break
down their rally stage in Lafayette Park near the White House
prematurely, but as police escorted them from the area, reports of
Antifa resistance emerged. Some 200 anti-fascists, many of them
wearing black masks, confronted police about a half-mile from the

White House as officers shoved them back, The Associated Press reported.

All rational people thanked the Police for their calm and professional way of dealing with what could have been a major incident.

At a news conference Sunday evening, Metropolitan Police Chief Peter Newsham said one man was arrested in connection with the protest. Newsham identified the man as 44-year-old John Mulligan of Pennsylvania and said he pepper-sprayed another man in the face at approximately 5 p.m., around the time the white nationalist demonstrators left Lafayette Park. The chief said Mulligan was carrying a slingshot, stones and large pieces of glass when he was apprehended.

Newsham rightfully praised his officers for showing "professionalism" and "class" when dealing with protesters on both sides and said, "we did not see any violent confrontations that we have seen in other cities."

Hours before this, the white nationalist rally participants -- a couple dozen in all, according to estimates -- gathered at a subway station in northern Virginia and traveled into the nation's capital via train before disembarking in Foggy Bottom near the George Washington University campus.

Police officers cleared a path through the counterprotesters for the group to march through on their way to Lafayette Park outside the White House. The far-right rallygoers marched in the middle of the street, surrounded by a big load of police, while counter-protesters heckled them from the sidewalks on either side.

While the far-right group held its rally in Lafayette Park, Antifa and Black Lives Matter protesters marched in the surrounding streets. At one point, an eruption of smoke emerged near the Eisenhower Executive Office Building next to the White House.

When the far-right group arrived at Lafayette Park, another large crowd greeted them with boos, cries of "shame," and chants of "Nazis go home" and "you are not welcome here."

"Unite the Right" organizer Jason Kessler said he expected 100 to 400 people to participate in the Lafayette Park event. However, their numbers appeared to be far fewer than that.

Some leading figures in the U.S. white nationalist movement said they would not attend or encouraged supporters to stay away.

By mid-afternoon, more than 1,000 people had gathered in Freedom Plaza, also near the White House, to oppose Kessler's demonstration. The counter-protesters planned to march to Lafayette Square just before the arrival of the white nationalists.

Makia Green, who represents the Washington branch of Black Lives Matter, told Sunday's crowd that: "We know from experience that ignoring white nationalism doesn't work." Amazing how she got the microphone. White Nationalism is not the side whites are taking nor is Antifa. Why not the side of stopping the crap and the hate.

Earlier in August 2018, Facebook stunned and angered counterprotester organizers when it disabled their Washington event's page, saying it and others had been created by "bad actors" misusing the social media platform. The company said at the time that the page may be linked to an account created by Russia's Internet Research Agency -- a so-called troll farm that has sown discord in the U.S. -- but counterprotesters said it was an authentic event they worked hard to organize.

Sunday Aug 12, 2018 marked one year after the original "Unite the Right" rally in Charlottesville, when hundreds of white nationalists — including neo-Nazis and Ku Klux Klan members — descended on Charlottesville in part to protest the city's decision to remove a monument to Confederate Gen. Robert E. Lee from a park.

Violent fighting broke out between attendees and counterprotesters in 2017. Authorities eventually forced the crowd to disperse, but a car later barreled into the crowd of peaceful counterprotesters, killing 32-year-old Heather Heyer, and injuring dozens more. A state police helicopter later crashed, killing two troopers.

This weekend was much quieter in Charlottesville. On Sunday morning, a crowd of more than 200 people gathered in a park to protest racism and remember Heyer. The group sang songs, and speakers addressed the crowd.

Authorities in Charlottesville confirmed that four people had been arrested, including a man and a woman who got into a fight after the man saluted the Lee statue.

Martin Clevenger, 29, of Spotsylvania, Va., and 40-year-old Veronica Fitzhugh, 40, of Charlottesville, were arrested on one count each of disorderly conduct and later released on a summons. When individual names are part of the story, you know the event was not a big deal, But the MSM, hungry for a story will make it the important news of the day simply because they can.

Another Charlottesville resident, 42-year-old Jesse Beard, was arrested on one count of obstruction of free passage and was released on a summons. Chloe Lubin, 29, of Portland, Maine, was arrested on charges of misdemeanor assault and battery, disorderly conduct, obstruction of justice and possession of a concealed weapon.

Authorities said Lubin spit in one demonstrator's face and clung on to another demonstrator as police tried to arrest her. She was later released on an unsecured bond.

On Saturday night, University of Virginia students and other activists briefly confronted police over the heavy security presence at a rally. They unfurled a banner reading, "Last year they came w/ torches. This year they come w/ badges" and chanted, "Why are you in riot gear? We don't see no riot here." More than 200 marched to another part of campus, where many shouted at a line of officers.

Fox News' Peter Doocy and Sarah Tobiankski in Washington and The Associated Press contributed to this report.

Chapter 14 Final Thoughts: Why a Nation in Turmoil Must Choose Civility

Aug 10th, 2018

Kay Coles James, President of The Heritage Foundation

COMMENTARY BY

James is a leader in government, academia and the conservative movement.

About the picture: Instead of ugly rancor, we should show respect. Instead of closed minds, we should have open hearts. And when called on to do so, we need to demonstrate our own quiet courage Kay James is the author of this piece on civility.

LoveTheWind/Getty Images

The three key takeaways outlined by Heritage for this insightful piece are as follows:

TAKEAWAYS

- ✓ With the nation in turmoil, 25 other black students and I helped integrate an all-white junior high school.

- ✓ Angry crowds that heckle and threaten are not trying to change hearts and win minds they're trying to impose their will through intimidation.

- ✓ With the nation once again in turmoil, more Americans in public and in private life alike need to choose civility.

In 1961, I participated in what a Richmond, Va., newspaper called "one of the most ambitious experiments in race-mixing the South had seen." With the nation in turmoil, 25 other black students and I helped integrate an all-white junior high school.

Outside the school, we faced angry crowds determined to prevent us from getting a quality education in peace. Inside, we were constantly afraid of being confronted by the white toughs who took special joy in threatening us black kids. We were just 12 years old at the time, and we felt outnumbered, intimidated and overwhelmed.

I'll never forget the day one of them made good on his threats. I was descending a large stairway when he pushed me from behind hard. I fell down the stone stairs, landing at the bottom with my shins and back badly bruised. Not done, the bully kicked my books all over the hall as his friends heckled and laughed at me.

And that's when an amazing thing happened.

One of the white girls in the crowd stepped forward and began helping me gather my books. She continued even as her friends turned on her and called her horrible names. Unfazed, she walked me down the hall to the nurse's office. She didn't say much, but she said enough to make it clear the boy who pushed me didn't speak or act for her and many others like her.

I've thought of that girl a lot this summer. Because her courage and kindness are so at odds with what's happened to Kirstjen Nielsen, Mitch McConnell and Brett Kavanaugh.

Nielsen is the secretary of Homeland Security. As such, she has been directly involved in one of the hottest issues of the day: illegal immigration. On June 20, she was quietly eating dinner at a D.C. restaurant when members of the Democratic Socialists of America approached her table and started chanting and heckling her. "Fascist pig!" one called her. "You're a villain!" another yelled. And then they ran her out of the restaurant.

Senate Majority Leader McConnell, R-Ky., found himself is a similar situation on several occasions. In addition to the name-calling and insults, he received an ominous threat: "We know where you live!" one protester bellowed.

Sadly, this behavior is being encouraged by some of our leaders. For example, Rep. Maxine Waters, D-Calif., told agitators, "If you see anybody from that Cabinet in a restaurant, in a department store, at a gasoline station, you get out and you create a crowd and you push back on them, and you tell them they're not welcome anymore, anywhere."

Now, being able to learn in peace and being able to eat or shop in peace are obviously different things. But there are unsettling similarities, too.

Angry crowds that heckle and threaten are not trying to change hearts and win minds they're trying to impose their will through intimidation. Worse, they can easily become violent.

It shouldn't, and doesn't have to, be this way. When I was attacked in that school stairwell, a brave girl stepped forward. Her quiet act of courage revealed her good heart and the power of civility. We need much, much more of that today.

July 12 marked the second annual "National Day of Civility," but there was precious little of it to be found in Washington that day. As Supreme Court nominee Brett Kavanaugh was introducing himself to senators, his opponents hurled incredibly insulting rhetoric at him.

Judge Kavanaugh is widely known for his intelligence, fairness, impartiality, and faithfulness to the Constitution. But that didn't stop radicals from smearing him as "intellectually and morally bankrupt." They were joined by former Virginia Gov. Terry McAuliffe, who said Kavanaugh's nomination "will threaten the lives of millions of Americans." Hollywood types weighed in, too, warning that Kavanaugh's confirmation would herald "the first American dictatorship."

And these are just a few of the many uncivil things said about this very civil jurist.

My friend Donna Brazile once said, "A government of, by, and for the people requires that people talk to people, that we can agree to disagree but do so in civility." Donna and I disagree about many approaches to public policy. But we strongly agree about being able to do so in a calm, respectful and civil manner.

With the nation once again in turmoil, more Americans in public and in private life alike need to choose civility. Instead of ugly rancor, we should show respect. Instead of closed minds, we should have open hearts. And when called on to do so, we need to demonstrate our own quiet courage.

It worked in a Richmond stairway. Isn't it time we try it as a nation? This piece originally appeared in Chicago Tribune

---

The Heritage Foundation is a great organization and its leader black conservative leader Kay Cole James is one of the best the organization could have selected for today's difficult mission. James knows a lot from personal discrimination—some from being a black lady and a ton more for being a conservative. Even the Trump White House missed out on James for an executive position because one of their top staff people rejected James. Here is that story:

With all the fawning the press is giving former Trump aide Omarosa, I thought this story might even up the score:

Heritage Foundation President Kay Coles James says she was "blocked" from serving in President Donald Trump's administration by Omarosa Manigault Newman, the former White House aide and reality television star.

"It was Omarosa," James said in an interview on POLITICO's Women Rule podcast that aired Wednesday, discussing how she has not managed to land a job in the administration despite her conservative bona fides.

"The way it was described to me is she approached the whole thing like it was 'The Apprentice,'" James added. "So she looked around Washington and said, 'OK, who do I need to get rid of first?'"

Manigault Newman, a former "Apprentice" star and vocal Trump surrogate in 2016, was the highest-ranking African-American adviser in the White House, serving as director of communications for the Office of Public Liaison. She announced her resignation from the post late last year, though reports later suggested she had been fired from the West Wing after butting heads with chief of staff John Kelly.

Trump's White House has been rapped for a lack of diversity and for having few women in senior positions, especially with the exits of Manigault Newman and Hope Hicks, the communications director. Critics also say the administration has experienced turmoil because Trump brought in many inexperienced Washington hands.

Trump lost a good one in Kay Cole James. Amarosa was anything but perfect.

Other Books by Brian Kelly: (amazon.com, and Kindle)

It's Time for The John Doe Party... Don't you think? By By Elephants.
Great Players in Florida Gators Football... Tim Tebow and a ton of other great players
Great Coaches in Florida Gators Football... The best coaches in Gator history.
The Constitution by Hamilton, Jefferson, Madison, et al. The Real Constitution
The Constitution Companion. Will help you learn and understand the Constitution
Great Coaches in Clemson Football The best Clemson Coaches right to Dabo Sinney
Great Players in Clemson Football The best Clemson players in history
Winning Back America. America's been stolen and can be won back completely
The Founding of America... Great book to pick up a lot of great facts
Defeating America's Career Politicians. The scoundrels need to go.
Midnight Mass by Jack Lammers... You remember what it was like Hreat story
The Bike by Jack Lammers... Great heartwarming Story by Jack
Wipe Out All Student Loan Debt--Now! Watch the economy go boom!
No Free Lunch Pay Back Welfare! Why not pay it back?
Deport All Millennials Now!!! Why they deserve to be deported and/or saved
DELETE the EPA, Please! The worst decisions to hurt America
Taxation Without Representation 4th Edition Should we throw the TEA overboard again?
Four Great Political Essays by Thomas Dawson
Top Ten Political Books for 2018... Cliffnotes Version of 10 Political Books
Top Six Patriotic Books for 2018... Cliffnotes version of 6 Patriotic Boosk
Why Trump Got Elected!.. It's great to hear about a great milestone in America!
The Day the Free Press Died. Corrupt Press Lives on!
Solved (Immigration) The best solutions for 2018
Solved II (Obamacare, Social Security, Student Debt) Check it out; They're solved.
Great Moments in Pittsburgh Steelers Football... Six Super Bowls and more.
Great Players in Pittsburgh Steelers Football ,,,Chuck Noll, Bill Cowher, Mike Tomin, etc.
Great Coaches in New England Patriots Football,,, Bill Belichick the one and only plus others
Great Players in New England Patriots Football... Tom Brady, Drew Bledsoe et al.
Great Coaches in Philadelphia Eagles Football..Andy Reid, Doug Pederson & Lots more
Great Players in Philadelphia Eagles Football Great players such as Sonny Jurgenson
Great Coaches in Syracuse Football All the greats including Ben Schwartzwalder
Great Players in Syracuse Football. Highlights best players such as Jim Brown & Donovan McNabb
Millennials are People Too !!! Give US millennials help to live American Dream
Brian Kelly for the United States Senate from PA: Fresh Face for US Senate
The Candidate's Bible. Don't pray for your campaign without this bible
Rush Limbaugh's Platform for Americans... Rush will love it
Sean Hannity's Platform for Americans... Sean will love it
Donald Trump's New Platform for Americans. Make Trump unbeatable in 2020
Tariffs Are Good for America! One of the best tools a president can have
Great Coaches in Pittsburgh Steelers Football Sixteen of the best coaches ever to coach in pro football.
Great Moments in New England Patriots Football Great football moments from Boston to New England
Great Moments in Philadelphia Eagles Football. The best from the Eagles from the beginning of football.
Great Moments in Syracuse Football The great moments, coaches & players in Syracuse Football
Boost Social Security Now! Hey Buddy Can You Spare a Dime?
The Birth of American Football. From the first college game in 1869 to the last Super Bowl
Obamacare: A One-Line Repeal Congress must get this done.
A Wilkes-Barre Christmas Story A wonderful town makes Christmas all the better
A Boy, A Bike, A Train, and a Christmas Miracle A Christmas story that will melt your heart
Pay-to-Go   America-First Immigration Fix
Legalizing Illegal Aliens Via Resident Visas Americans-first plan saves $Trillions. Learn how!
60 Million Illegal Aliens in America!!! A simple, America-first solution.
The Bill of Rights By Founder James Madison Refresh *your knowledge of the specific rights for all*
Great Players in Army Football Great Army Football played by great players..
Great Coaches in Army Football Army's coaches are all great.
Great Moments in Army Football Army Football at its best.
Great Moments in Florida Gators Football Gators Football from the start. This is the book.
Great Moments in Clemson Football CU Football at its best. This is the book.
Great Moments in Florida Gators Football Gators Football from the start. This is the book.
The Constitution Companion. A Guide to Reading and Comprehending the Constitution
The Constitution by Hamilton, Jefferson, & Madison – Big type and in English

PATERNO: The Dark Days After Win # 409. Sky began to fall within days of win # 409.
JoePa 409 Victories: Say No More! Winningest Division I-A football coach ever
American College Football: The Beginning From before day one football was played.
Great Coaches in Alabama Football Challenging the coaches of every other program!
Great Coaches in Penn State Football the Best Coaches in PSU's football program
Great Players in Penn State Football The best players in PSU's football program
Great Players in Notre Dame Football The best players in ND's football program
Great Coaches in Notre Dame Football The best coaches in any football program
Great Players in Alabama Football from Quarterbacks to offensive Linemen Greats!
Great Moments in Alabama Football AU Football from the start. This is the book.
Great Moments in Penn State Football PSU Football, start--games, coaches, players,
Great Moments in Notre Dame Football ND Football, start, games, coaches, players
Cross Country with the Parents A great trip from East Coast to West with the kids
Seniors, Social Security & the Minimum Wage. Things seniors need to know.
How to Write Your First Book and Publish It with CreateSpace
The US Immigration Fix--It's all in here. Finally, an answer.
I had a Dream IBM Could be #1 Again The title is self-explanatory
WineDiets.Com Presents The Wine Diet Learn how to lose weight while having fun.
Wilkes-Barre, PA; Return to Glory Wilkes-Barre City's return to glory
Geoffrey Parsons' Epoch... The Land of Fair Play Better than the original.
The Bill of Rights 4 Dummmies! This is the best book to learn about your rights.
Sol Bloom's Epoch …Story of the Constitution The best book to learn the Constitution
America 4 Dummmies! All Americans should read to learn about this great country.
The Electoral College 4 Dummmies! How does it really work?
The All-Everything Machine Story about IBM's finest computer server.
ThankYou IBM! This book explains how IBM was beaten in the computer marketplace by neophytes

Brian has written 173 books in total. Other books can be found at amazon.com/author/brianwkelly